MARTIN H. SCHARLEMANN

Proclaiming the Parables

THE WITNESSING CHURCH SERIES
William J. Danker, Editor

CONCORDIA PUBLISHING HOUSE
SAINT LOUIS, MISSOURI

Concordia Publishing House, Saint Louis, Missouri 63118
Copyright 1963 by Concordia Publishing House

Library of Congress Catalog Card No. 63-12300

Manufactured in the United States of America

4 5 6 7 8 9 10 11 12   V P   91 90 89 88

FOREWORD

One of the very hopeful signs in Christendom is the renaissance of Biblical studies in all sectors of the church, including both Protestant and Roman circles.

New light has been shed by archaeological and historical studies on the meaning of the New Testament and its production by human instruments in a Christian community under the guidance of the Holy Spirit, who thus communicated Himself to them and brought to remembrance all the mighty acts of God now seen in their true significance from a vantage point on this side of Bethlehem, Calvary, the open tomb, the Ascension, and Pentecost.

After a century of such Biblical scholarship, including careful many-faceted investigations of the entire milieu in which the Biblical writings were produced, a whole new set of tools is at hand for the preacher who truly desires to dig into the Scriptures. Here we recall Dr. Ludwig Fuerbringer's occasional references to the Norwegian Bible translation which renders "Search the Scriptures," "Ransack the Scriptures" — for the purpose of discovering a fuller, more faithful, more flavorful understanding of what the Holy Spirit is saying to us through His inspired Word. It is possible that we do not yet know all the uses of these tools. For many pastors, even for specialists, there simply has not been time to grow skillful and adept in the full use of all these digging instruments. And since human beings are fallible, it is, of course, possible for accidents to happen as people use these tools. They are sharp, and some are double-edged. On occasion, instead of slitting open the Scriptural meaning, it is possible to cut oneself instead.

But hazard has always attended the study of Scripture. Second Peter calls attention to this in speaking of Paul's letters: ". . . they contain some obscure passages which the ignorant and unstable misinterpret to their own ruin as they do the other Scriptures." (2 Peter 3:16, NEB)

Finally, any instruments of Biblical study will have to prove themselves in action. Do they help one better to understand what the Lord of history has caused to be put into His Holy Word? Do they help us better to apply these messages to our time? The proof of the pudding will be in the eating, not in the recitation of the recipe. The strength of this treatise is its sincere and constructive endeavor to demonstrate the positive, affirmative use of current Biblical scholarship. Some have never given themselves a fair and honest chance to study the believing and loyal use of modern methods for Biblical scholarship or their merits in the light of Scriptural data and evidence. In a church whose boast is "Sola Scriptura" Biblical studies must ever reign supreme over systematic formulations. Where systems rule instead of the sovereign Word there is rigidity, sterility, and frequently a loss of missionary vitality.

Without a genuinely Biblical message of redemption through Jesus Christ and the proclamation of God's kingdom, mission work degenerates into mere activism. If the message runs thin, reliance on counseling and group dynamics are not going to hold the church together or launch the church like a thunderbolt at the vast missionary challenges of our time. Rich and relevant preaching is essential. We trust that under God's guidance and blessing the present essay will make a helpful contribution.

The pastors present for the sixth annual Parish Administration Institute at Concordia Seminary, St. Louis, Mo., earnestly requested the publication of what was originally a series of five lectures by Dr. Martin Scharlemann.

WILLIAM J. DANKER

January 10, 1963

CONTENTS

Foreword	3
Introduction	9
The Word "Parable"	13
The Interpretation of Parables	21
The Kingdom of God	31
The Automatic Action of the Soil	47
The Two Sons	57
The Barren Fig Tree	63
The Unjust Judge	73
The Unjust Manager	80

INTRODUCTION

Proclamation involves a message and a mission. As originally presented these discussions bore the heading "Mining the Message for the Mission." That wording underscores the fundamental business of the church in the two words "message" and "mission," as well as the prior responsibility of the proclaimer, that of mining the proclamation we are to "sound out" to lost mankind. This *kerygma*, as Professor Dodd has taught us to call it, is nowhere more eloquently and succinctly given than in the parables of Jesus. We trust, therefore, it will be of service to our fellow proclaimers — and this includes all Christians — to send forth this study of the parabolic teaching of our Lord and Savior.

It may be useful to state the sequence of steps which comprise the process of mining, reminding ourselves that behind any thorough study of the text are to be found the painstaking and often tedious "digging" efforts of the interpreter. We are accustomed to spell out the task of mining the text as follows:

1. Establish the correct text (critical apparatus)

2. Know each word (lexicon)
3. Know each grammatical form (grammar)
4. Relate phrases and sentences to each other (particles; participles; subordination; coordination) (syntax)
5. Write out a rough translation
6. Determine the thought progression in the text
7. Relate the passage to the context (near and remote)
8. Relate the text to the unifying theme of Scripture
9. Do a word study of the main concepts (concordance)
10. Look at other translations
11. Prepare your own final translation
12. Ruminate (write out thoughts as they come to you while you are reflecting on the text)
13. Select the key thought and formulate it as the central thought (i. e., combine the text with the need to which you are addressing yourself)
14. Establish the logical divisions of the central thought
15. Write out an outline

We shall not go through each of these steps individually in this presentation. We shall, however, attempt to take the reader from text to outline on the basis of our own private mining of the texts selected for our study. Before taking up these readings, however, it will be necessary to present a brief study of the term "parable" as the Scriptures use this world. In that connection we shall find it useful to discuss the purpose of parabolic teaching and to indicate the approximate number of parables to be found in the Synoptic Gospels. Since the parables describe certain aspects of the kingdom of God, we cannot escape the responsibility of clarifying this particular concept in the light of God's dealings with Israel and His creation of the church. Nor can we avoid giving some thought to the knotty problem of interpreting the parables properly.

Only then shall we proceed to take up certain selected parables, in this instance the following five:

Automatic Action of the Soil (The Seed Growing Secretly)	Mark 4:26-29
The Two Sons	Matt. 21:28-32
The Barren Fig Tree	Luke 13:6-9
The Unjust Judge	Luke 18:1-8
The Unjust Manager	Luke 16:1-13

The treatment of each parable is divided into three parts: textual, exegetical, and homiletical. Whatever sermon outlines are included are offered with great hesitation, on the realization that no two people work the same way and that one man's outline may be utterly useless to another person. Possibly they can serve best as a brief summary of what is to be found in the respective parables under discussion.

We seek to attain three major objectives:

1. Provide the opportunity for developing an understanding of the concept of the kingdom of God as it occurs in the parables of Jesus;

2. Provide the opportunity for developing an appreciation of the parables of Jesus as a primary instrument for proclaiming the kingdom of God;
3. Offer the occasion for developing a sense of gratitude to God for having revealed Himself to us through His Son as determined and active in reestablishing His rule over and among men through His Son.

The literature available on the subject of parables is vast. Much of it is out of date. A brief bibliography is appended, therefore, for the guidance and interest of anyone willing to pursue the study of parables beyond the area covered by the present series.

C. H. Dodd, *Parables of the Kingdom* (London: Nisbet & Company, 1960 revision)

A. M. Hunter, *Interpreting the Parables* (Philadelphia: Westminster, 1960)

Joachim Jeremias, *The Parables of Jesus* (London: SCM Press, 1954)

Wilhelm Michaelis, *Die Gleichnisse Jesu* (Hamburg: Im Furche Verlag, 1956)

Franz M. Moschner, *The Kingdom of Heaven in Parables* (St. Louis: B. Herder, 1960)

THE WORD "PARABLE"

A study of some of the parables of Jesus is an undertaking that merits our effort and attention. For one thing, no less than one third of the recorded teaching of Jesus consists of parables. This consideration alone would make it inviting and necessary to give some thought to this element of the Synoptic Gospels. Moreover, the parables are unique in their content. They constitute an original factor in our Lord's instructional activity. Even the most rabid form critic will concede that in the parables of Jesus we touch upon a basic stratum of what we know about Jesus of Nazareth. Again, the parables describe the kingdom of God in action. They do not deal with abstract truths. They are descriptive, telling us of something that happens when God is busy reestablishing Himself as King among and over men. Small wonder that the parables constitute something of a touchstone for understanding Jesus' proclamation, "The kingdom of God is at hand." We might add that there is power in the present-day use of parables. A person who hears or reads a parable of Jesus is confronted by the necessity of making up his mind about Jesus Himself.

It is not enough to know the customs and practices of Palestine in the first century of our era. After all, no one was more familiar with these matters than the contemporaries of Jesus. Nevertheless, they did not understand the parables. For a mysterious element pervades our Lord's parabolic instructives. P. G. Wodehouse at one place makes one of his characters say that "a parable is one of those stories in the Bible which sounds like a pleasant yarn but keeps something up its sleeve which pops up and leaves you flat." This is a very apt description of a very elusive quality about the parables. Finally, we need to note that many of the parables of Jesus occur in the standard pericopes of the regular church year. It should be helpful, therefore, for our preaching to become acquainted in greater detail with a few of the parables and some of the matters which surround their interpretation and understanding.

The word "parable" belongs to the language of revelation. Like "grace" and "faith" it belongs to the lexicon of "good news"; it is descriptive of God's activity rather than being either prescriptive or predictive. It is a kerygmatic term in the fullest sense of the word.

The Greek *parabole* occurs only in the Synoptics and in Hebrews. The evangelist John does not use it even when it might be expected, as in John 10:6, where the King James translation reads: "This parable spake Jesus unto them, but they understood not what things they were which He spake unto them." The word used in the fourth Gospel is *paroimia* rather than *parabole*. There are two occurrences of the term "parable" in the epistle to the Hebrews, namely, at 9:9 and 11:19. There, however, it has quite a different meaning. In the first of these, the Revised Standard Version has "symbolic"; in the second context, it is translated "figuratively." In neither instance does it refer to a form of discourse. Outside of Hebrews, therefore, *parabole* is used only in the first three Gospels; and there it appears in no less than 48 instances. Matthew uses it 17 times, Mark gives it 13 times, and Luke employs it 18 times.

It is evident both from the usage of the word in the Synoptics and from a direct statement of Matthew (13:34-35) that the term *parabole* is closely related to the Septuagint use of the same word as a translation for *mashal*. Matthew alludes to Ps. 78:2, where the Greek Old Testament uses just this word, describing Jesus as using parables in fulfillment of the Old Testament passage. It is of importance to realize that the translators of the Greek Old Testament used *parabole* for the Hebrew *mashal*. One might expect that fables such as those told by Jotham (Judg. 9:8-20) and Jehoash (2 Kings 14:9) might be spoken of as "parables." One might also look for the word in connection with the riddle of Samson (Judg. 14:14), or the teaching of Nathan (2 Sam. 12:1 ff.). However, it is not found there. It is used rather as a concept which formed part of the Old Testament idea of wisdom or of revelation.

The dark and mysterious pronouncements of Balaam in Num. 23:7; 23:18; 24:3 and 24:15-23 are called *parabolai*. The word is also used of short proverbs, as in 1 Sam. 10:12. The Book of Proverbs carries the title *Meshalim*, which is translated in the Vulgate, for example, as *Parabolai*, although the Septuagint has *Paroimiai* here. Prov. 1:6 uses *mashal* to describe an enigmatic maxim. The term is also used of some of the allegories found in the Book of Ezekiel, although there, too, it leans toward the meaning of proverb rather than of a comparison (cf. Ezek. 12:22, 23). It is not quite accurate, therefore, to say, as Juelicher did, that the most which can be done is to say that the Old Testament *mashal* is a discourse expressing or implying a comparison. In the Old Testament the thought of similarity is very frequently subordinated, if not almost lost completely, to the idea of mysterious or prophetic utterance. From the Septuagint it is clear that the word *parabole* is part of the terminology of that miraculous process known as God's revelation of Himself.

The idea of comparison seems to become part of the term in the centuries just prior to the New Testament age. The Greeks understood *parabole* as meaning an analogy. Aristotle uses it in this sense, when he describes Socrates as likening political elections by the *demos* to the practice of naval crews selecting their own officers. This sense is derived from the etymology of the term. The verb *paraballomai* means "to throw next to," "to line up" — as ships in battle! In Hellenistic Greek *parabole* retains this significance. Moulton and Milligan, in their *Vocabulary of the Greek New Testament*, quote Quintillian as saying that Cicero called a *parabole* a *collatio*. In the New Testament this thought of similarity is retained in places. Jesus began many of His parables with the statement, "The kingdom of God is like unto." However, even here the overtones of mystery and revelation sound rather loudly. There is not the slightest hint of a comparison in the use of the word as it is found, for example, at Luke 4:23, where it refers to the proverb, "Physician, heal thyself."

There are other contexts, however, where *parabolai* is used of what we might call similitudes *(Gleichnisse)*. In Matt. 24:32, for instance, we read the words of Jesus, "Learn of the fig tree . . ." as he poses a similarity between the signs that bespeak the coming of spring and the events preceding the second return of our Lord. Yet also here there is less emphasis on an analogous arrangement than on the prophetic nature of Jesus' utterance.

From all of these considerations it would seem that the term is used in the New Testament as part of the terminology applied to the instructional and revelatory activity of Jesus. He had come as priest and king, to be sure, but also as God's prophet, proclaiming the mystery of the kingdom. It is in this kind of context that the word *parabole* comes to life in the New Testament.

It is of some interest to note the verbs used in connection with the term "parable." *Paratithenai* has to do with setting a parable before a hearer. It suggests the picture described in Psalm 23, "Thou preparest a table before me in the presence of mine enemies." Here is further indication that *parabolai* is intended to be understood in terms of God's grace. Two words are used of the art of explaining parables. They are *diasaphein* and *phrazein*. The words for "knowing," "learning," and "inquiring" are all found in combinations with *parabolai*. They indicate the close relationship of the word to God's work of revealing Himself, suggesting that Christ came to be our wisdom. One of the means He used in revealing God's wisdom to us was parabolic teaching.

We often think of a parable as being a story that is or may not be true and is generally used to teach some religious truth. *The Westminster Dictionary of the Bible,* as a case in point, defines a parable as "a method of speech in which moral or religious truth is illustrated from the analogy of common experience." That, however, is only one meaning of the word. It has several others, both in the Old and in the New Testament. In the Old Testament, as we have indicated, the word is used of short proverbs, of mysterious utterances, of riddles or even of allegory. The same latitude is found in the New Testament, where, as we have seen, it connotes a short saying, or a mere comparison without a narrative. But it is employed also of comparisons extended into narratives. This is what we normally mean when we use the term "parable." In every instance, however, the thought of mystery is not far removed from the concept. This must be kept in mind as we look at some parables for what they say about the kingdom of God.

Oesterley distinguishes four types of parables within the Gospels: a simple saying; those which contain a comparison; those which contain an element of allegory; and finally, those stories which depict some aspect of God's kingdom. As one might expect, these four classes overlap to some extent. The distinction is made more for purposes of clarification than for strict classification. Because of the latitude in the use and meaning of the term, authorities differ as to the number of parables that are actually found in the Gospels. Von Koetsveld recognizes 79. He includes in this figure a number of sections from the Gospel of St. John. Bugge lists 71; Juelicher has 53; Smith, 62; Heinrichi, 39; Bruce, 33 (plus eight "parable gems"). In his most recent book Archibald M. Hunter speaks of "about sixty." Moulton says that the widespread, less accurate enumeration of between 30 to 40 restricts the parable largely to story form. Trench lists 30 and C. H. Dodd mentions 44. The *Interpreter's Bible,* in an article by Walter Russel Bowie, lists 51 passages as parabolic. This very considerable divergence stems from the fact that the meaning of the word is not fully agreed upon and cannot be limited to one area. We must note, however, that some stories of the New Testament do not belong to the category of parables. They are only illustrative stories. The Good Samaritan as well as Dives and Lazarus belong to this category.

Recognizing this great diversity in the various listings given, it may be useful to put down those items about which there can be very little doubt. Three parables are found in all the Synoptic Gospels: the Sower; the Mustard Seed; and the Wicked Tenants. In Matthew and Luke we find two: the Leaven and the Lost Sheep. Matthew alone has the following: the Tares; the Hidden Treasure; the Pearl; the Net; the Unmerciful Servant; the Laborers in the Vineyard; the Two Sons; the Marriage of the King's Son; the Wise and Foolish Virgins; the Talents. The parable of the Automatic Action of the Soil is found only in Mark. Luke alone has the Rich Fool; the Barren Fig Tree; the Great Supper; the Lost Coin; the Prodigal Son; the Unjust Manager; the Unjust Judge; the Pharisee and the Publican; and the Pounds.

If these statistical observations sound rather elementary and uninspiring, let us remind ourselves that they help us to appreciate the diversity of treatment found in the Synoptics. Each evangelist reveals his own particular interests and emphases also in the way he records the parables of Jesus. Luke, for instance, gives us a considerable amount of parabolic instruction found neither in Mark nor in Matthew. Much of this is found in a long section describing Jesus' Perean ministry, to which the other two Synoptics hardly refer. These differences among the Synoptics must be taken into account in the study of any single parable.

THE INTERPRETATION OF PARABLES

The problem of interpreting the parables of Jesus is one that has received a great deal of attention throughout the history of the church. Different principles have been applied with varying results. Generally speaking, these approaches might be classified under the following five heads: analogy, generalization, setting in life, prophecy, and the principle of divine purpose in redemption. We shall take up each one of these in turn.

According to the principle of analogy parables are to be interpreted in the light of the conviction that the earthly story of a parable imperfectly reflects some heavenly counterpart. This is an application of an observation expressed in the lines from Milton's *Paradise Lost:*

... what if earth
Be but a shadow of heaven, and things therein
Each to the other like, more than on earth is thought?
(V, 575 ff.)

This is the principle which gave rise to the excesses of the allegorical method associated particularly with the ancient school of Alexandria. In this kind of treatment every detail of a parable often receives independent significance, a meaning quite apart from the main interest of the parable. In the early church this method was employed rather generally. Only the school of Antioch seems to have escaped the pitfalls created by this particular approach. Unfortunately, the school of Antioch was in time suspected of heretical leanings so that its influence on later centuries vanished. Alexandrian allegory, orginally applied to pagan Greek literature, dominated Christian exegetical activity well into the Middle Ages.

This cannot be the proper method of interpreting the parables because the Scriptures are very emphatic in their insistence that God is the Unfathomable. The principle of analogy is, in fact, neo-Platonic in conception and execution. It would be valid only on the basis of the assumption that there is a similarity between life here on earth and God's own being and activity. Something of the backwash of this methodology can be seen in Professor Dodd's statement: "Since nature and supernature are one order, you can take any part of that order and find in it illumination for the other part. . . . This sense of the divineness of the natural order is the major premise of all the parables" (p. 22). When approached in this way parables are seen as leading to a general truth that can be predicated both of the heavenly sphere and of our earthly existence. It may be worth pointing out that Trench's book on parables suffers from this tendency to allegorize.

The second principle is that of generalization. It is represented chiefly by Adolph Juelicher's monumental two volumes, *Die Gleichnisreden Jesu*. In this method the parables are no longer treated as establishing a comparison between two levels of existence, the earthly and the heavenly, but merely between two modes of experience. It denies the validity of the distinction between nature and supernature and is content to extract from the parables no more than general truisms.

Applying this principle to the parable of the Sower, for example, we would come up with the observation that any kind of religious work involves much loss of labor but that a good harvest results nevertheless. Or, to take another instance, the parable of the Treasure teaches that one should always sacrifice a lower good for a higher one. This kind of interpretation reduces the parables to being illustrations of eminently sound moral and religious principles but no more. One is left with the question whether our Lord told parables just to underscore certain general truths about life.

Although this method neglects the concrete details of the parable story completely, something wholesome has resulted from Juelicher's work. His volumes provided the kind of corrective that was needed in this field at the time. They helped to do away with the excesses of the allegorical method. But they went too far in their insistence that no parable contained allegorical elements of any kind. Juelicher denies that the interpretation of the Sower, with its allegorical features, actually comes from the lips of Jesus Himself. He holds that this explanation owes its form and content to the needs and interests of the early church. Now, it may well be that the interpretation as we have it was influenced by later concerns. However, to argue that it cannot be Jesus' own just because it contains allegorical elements certainly looks like a clear case of arguing in a circle.

There is another approach to the parables. It is that of form criticism, which proposes to strip away every accretion from the period of oral tradition and gospel composition. The best example of this methodology is to be found in *The Parables of Jesus* by Joachim Jeremias, which is devoted to determining the hermeneutical rules by which the interpreter can study a given parable in its original setting in the life of Jesus. Others, like Dodd, want to find the "setting in life" in the life of the early church. The chief virtue of this approach is its insistence on careful literary and theological analysis.

In this connection it may be of some interest to point out that the parables of Jesus, as they occur in the Synoptics, actually form three clusters. There are, first of all, the parables of growth that Jesus related toward the end of the first part of His Galilean ministry, when His clear sayings had been rejected by most of the people who had heard Him. The parables belonging to the second group are found for the most part in St. Luke. They propose to present various aspects and obligations of Christian living as such. The third cluster grew out of the activities and reactions of our Lord's ministry during Holy Week. These are for the most part parables of judgment.

It is certainly helpful to know this general distinction, which is derived from the framework of Jesus' own personal ministry as it is given by the Gospel accounts. However, what is usually meant by "setting in life" is the occasion and use of a particular parable in the history of the early church. Form critics who follow this particular method try to determine what part of the parable Jesus Himself actually related, and what elements were added later on by the church from her experience. The parable of the Unjust Steward (Luke 16:1-13) might be a case in point. According to the form critic approach, this parable probably ended with the sentence, "The Lord commended the unjust steward." To this parable the evangelist then added a series of lessons, which reflect at least three different interpretations given by the early church to this parable: first, the sons of this age are more prudent in relation to their own time than are the sons of life; secondly, make friends by means of unrighteous wealth; and thirdly, if you have not been honest with unrighteous wealth, who will entrust you with the true riches? Of this Dodd says, "We can almost see here notes of three separate sermons on the parable as a text" (p. 30).

One might observe at this point that no two form critics agree in their conclusions. Jeremias has applied this method about as consistently and thoroughly as one can imagine. His volume contains much that is constructive; and yet one must begin to wonder whether the original form of the parables can be fully determined at all. A good bit of historical information is obtained this way. But that will not essentially deepen our understanding and appreciation of the parables. Happily, many of the form critics themselves do not follow this method consistently. Dodd, for example, is honest enough to say in one place, "Any serious work of art has significance beyond its occasion" (p. 49). Despite his interest in form criticism, he interprets many of the parables on the principle that there is an identity of structure between the ministry of Jesus and the work of the church, and between the life of the first disciples and the believers of all generations.

Another method we have is called that of prophecy. In the eighteenth century it was represented by Vitringa's *Erklärung der Parabolen*, consisting of more than a thousand closely-printed pages. In Vitringa's view the servant owing the ten thousand talents (Matthew 18:23) is the pope, who misused his position of trust in the church and was warned by the invasion of Goths and other barbarians. But he was mercifully delivered by the Carlovingian kings. However, far from repenting and amending his ways, the papacy oppressed the true servants of God more than ever at the time of the Reformation. Nothing but irreversible doom awaited him now. Remnants of this method are found today in G. H. Lang's *The Parabolic Teaching of Scripture*. Here the parable of the Leaven is made to apply to the rise of "the vast hierarchical system of the papacy" (p. 103). Not much can be said for this approach. As in the instance of allegory, it is controlled and guided by little except the vagaries of the interpreter.

The final method is one that relates the parables of Jesus to the whole story of God's redemptive concern. This method recognizes the parables as being kerygmatic, as being told to call forth the recognition of Jesus as embodying in His person and ministry the powers of the kingdom of God. Accordingly, the parables constitute a touchstone of understanding the nature of God's kingdom as seen in the words and works of Jesus. The "mystery" referred to in Mark's statement on the purposes of the parables (4:11, 12) is none other than Jesus Himself. In Him God came to reestablish Himself as King in a very particular and final way. The parables confront the hearer and the reader with the challenge to take a position over against Jesus of Nazareth. They represent an invitation to decide for the Savior. He had come to redeem mankind; so He confronted men, particularly in the parables, with the necessity of accepting Him in order to make sense out of His parabolic teaching.

This way of interpreting the parables recognizes the difference between the heavenly and the earthly realms. It is agreed that there is no direct analogy between the two. The link that holds the two together can be found in the person and in the work of Jesus Christ. The parables, then, must be seen in the light of the total activity and message of the Lord. The peculiar characteristic of the parables, in distinction from the plain sayings of Jesus, is just this that they demand, to an even higher degree, a knowledge and acceptance of the total redemptive activity of God in history. A parable confronts the hearer with the question as to whether he wants an explanation of the story told; and the only way of receiving an answer is that of coming into closer relationship with the author of the parables.

As in the instance of all the sayings of Jesus the reaction to the parables He related was a twofold one. A separation took place among the hearers. There were those who accepted Jesus; for them the parables became a vehicle for clarification. On the other hand, there were those who rejected Him. In that case the parables became a means for obscuring the truth. The casual hearer, however, would be led to inquire further into the significance of the story told. In this respect parables served a purpose beyond that of the direct sayings of Jesus.

In the actual technique of interpreting a parable we must distinguish between the point of comparison and the central truth. The latter is derived from the former. Perhaps an illustration will serve our purpose best. In the instance of the Unmerciful Servant (Matt. 18:23-35) the *tertium comparationis* might be worded as follows: God withdraws His offer of forgiveness when men fail to forgive others, even as the king of the parable withdrew his cancellation of the servant's huge debt. The central truth would read: Let us forgive others as God has forgiven us.

Normally a parable has but one main point. The details of the story have no independent significance of their own. They must be subordinated to the chief point. Therefore, normally only those details can be interpreted which are affected by the point of similarity. George Hubbard once remarked, "A parable is like a lens which gathers many of the sun's rays and brings them to focus on a single point. It is like a circle with many radii of detail meeting at the center, and this center it is which the expositor is concerned to find." It is this central focus which most distinguishes the parables from allegory; for in allegory every detail has a significance of its own.

Now, when it comes to the application of this observation we shall discover that the parables of Jesus fall into four general categories. There are those in which no details or very few have any significance. In other instances a goodly number of details can be used in the interpretation of the parables. Some parables, in the third instance, are of the kind where almost all of the details have a significant relationship to the major point. Finally, there are a few parables in which a second independent thought is presented, almost on the same level with the first point of comparison.

Since it is of primary importance to arrive at the point of comparison, we face the question of a precise method for reaching this kernel and of being reasonably sure of its identification. The following suggestions may be helpful in this connection. It is certainly essential to be familiar with the social and cultural conditions prevailing at the time of Jesus. It is only necessary to call attention to this matter in connection with the parable of the Wise and Foolish Virgins to realize how much a full comprehension of the parable and its point of comparison depends on our understanding the marital customs of that day. Furthermore, a general appreciation of agricultural methods is certainly a prerequisite for understanding the parable of the Sower. At the same time we must point out that the people who knew the practices and customs of that day best were contemporaries of our Lord; and yet most of them did not penetrate to the significance of His parables. They would not accept Jesus; and so all things happened to them in riddles. (Mark 4:12)

Again, certain concepts that occur in the parables are explained in the Gospel accounts. These must be taken into consideration. For instance, we are told what we are to understand by the seed, the harvest, the net, and the soil. Where these explanations occur they help us in determining the point of comparison in a given instance.

Moreover, in many instances the context of a parable is helpful in arriving at the *tertium*. For instance, the parable of the Lost Sheep must most certainly be interpreted in the light of the first two verses of Luke 15, where we are told that Jesus ate with publicans and sinners and the scribes and Pharisees complained about his associations with these people. In the light of its surroundings, this parable was told to underline the joy of our heavenly Father at the sight of a repentant sinner.

Finally, we must be aware of the fact that parables cannot be used to develop theological arguments. They are not armories for forging theological weapons. Their purpose is to illustrate and fortify Scriptural teaching. "Theologia parabolica non est theologia argumentativa," is the way this observation was put in days gone by.

In all this it is of fundamental importance to remember that the parables of Jesus were spoken to ordinary folk. They were related to be understood by even the most simple person, if and when he stood in a relationship of faith in Jesus as the embodiment of God's kingdom. The parables of Jesus are given in our Synoptic Gospels as a source of information and inspiration for the most childlike trust. Their interpretation, therefore, ought not to be complicated and intricate. The advice of John Chrysostom is still relevant at this point, "Don't overwork the details of the parable." This practical suggestion might be put more colloquially as follows, "Don't make a parable walk on all fours."

THE KINGDOM OF GOD

It is evident from Matt. 25:34 that the kingdom of God belongs to that plan of our heavenly Father which He designed from all eternity as our way of salvation. For there the Son of man, returning for judgment, is described as saying to those on His right, "Come, O blessed of my Father, inherit the kingdom prepared for you from the foundation of the world." This kingdom was historically realized, in a most striking manner, for the first time at Mount Sinai. To be sure, God had tried at the time of Noah to begin anew with a single family. But man's pride and sin kept excluding the rule of God from the affairs of men, as witness the attempt to build the Tower of Babel. It was then that God chose Abraham to be the father of a new kind of people.

In time God began to implement His choice of Israel. He dealt with it by way of the exodus of the Israelites and the creation of a covenant at Mount Sinai. Here Israel is specifically referred to as a kingdom, in the words of Ex. 19:5, 6: "Now, therefore, if you will obey My voice and keep My covenant, you shall be My own possession among all peoples; for all the earth is Mine, and you shall be to Me a kingdom of priests, and a holy nation."

This is as close as the Old Testament ever gets to the expression "kingdom of God." To be sure, in the later chapters of Isaiah and in some of the Psalms we find the verbal combination, "God rules." The noun form of this, however, does not occur until the intertestamental period. It was then that the scribes and the rabbis began to speak of the kingdom of God. In fact some of them went so far as to say that no prayer was complete without some reference to this kingdom, the *malkuth*, as they called it.

We speak of this as the kingdom of God because the Lord Himself created it. He chose to enter into a special relationship with His people Israel. It became His son, His firstborn (Ex. 4:22). That is to say, the God of all nations decided to be identified in His redemptive purposes with this lowly race of slaves.

Pharaoh might well boast, "Who is the Lord that I should obey Him?" Nevertheless, at the Red Sea this Lord manifested His power in such a way as to make it very clear not only to Pharaoh but also to His people that He was indeed the Lord of history, who had taken a direct hand in the affairs of men to make one nation His very own. He did so not because there was anything special about Israel. As a matter of fact, in the seventh chapter of Deuteronomy we are reminded that God chose Israel only because He loved her. There we read (vv. 7, 8 RSV): "It was not because you were more in number than any other people that the Lord set His love upon you and chose you, for you were the fewest of all peoples; but it is because the Lord loves you, and is keeping the oath which He swore to your fathers, that the Lord has brought you out with a mighty hand, and redeemed you from the house of bondage, from the hand of Pharaoh, king of Egypt."

It is the very nature of that God whom we know from the Scriptures to associate Himself with the lowly. St. Paul reminds us of this in the opening chapter of First Corinthians, saying (v. 28): "God chose what is low and despised in the world, even things that are not, to bring to nothing things that are. . . ." In the preface to his commentary on the Magnificat, Luther has a precious statement on this point. There he makes the point that God cannot look above Himself; for there is none greater than He. He cannot look next to Himself, because there is none like Him. The only place He can look is down below; and the lower we are the better He can see us. On this basis God chose Mary as the mother of His Son. Israel became God's people on the same principle of grace. Left on our own, we would very likely have proceeded differently. We might have selected either Assyria or Egypt, possibly even Greece, as the nation likely to be most suited to carry out God's purposes. But Israel's Lord, and ours, has His own way of doing things — dealing with men in mercy and grace rather than in response to their achievements. "For it is the nature of the divine will, according to 1 Samuel 2:6," as Luther reminds us, "that 'it kills and makes alive, that it brings down to hell and brings back again.' This means: it does good by doing us harm, it is most acceptable when it causes our displeasure, and it perfects while it destroys" (*Luther: Lectures on Romans,* Westminster, 1961, p. 331).

We may therefore call grace the first characteristic of the kingdom of God. God's kingdom does not come in response to man's achievement. It is entirely God's own creation. In time the Jews forgot this very important point, despite the fact that their prophets and their Scriptures kept reminding them of God's undeserved favor as manifested in the story of God's dealings with Israel.

As a second feature of this kingdom we might list the fact that God chose to dwell with His people. The book of Exodus begins with the story of Israel's redemption from Egypt and ends with the erection of the tabernacle, the tent of meeting. Here was the place that the God whom "the heaven and the heaven of heavens cannot contain" deigned to use as the place of His gracious presence. At three points in particular God chose to meet His people in the tabernacle. Of the mercy seat (Ex. 25:22) God said, "There I will meet with thee to speak there unto thee." He used the same expression with reference to the altar of burnt offering (Ex. 29:42) and of the altar of incense (Ex. 30:6). Israel therefore became the people of God's presence. This means that the Lord of heaven and earth invaded the realm of time and space to move with His nation through the desert into the Promised Land. He is not a god like those of the heathen nations, bound to one mountain or to one shrine. Many years later God reminded David through Nathan,

"I have not dwelt in a house since the day I brought up the people of Israel from Egypt to this day, but I have been moving about in a tent for My dwelling" (2 Sam. 7:6).

We must also point out that Israel was designed as a community set apart to do God's will. Have you not often wondered about the many rules and regulations given especially in the book of Leviticus? These were intended to serve as a reminder to the Israelites that they were God's people indeed. At every turn in life they were alerted by these laws to the fact that their task was to do God's will. To make it possible for anyone who transgressed these ordinances to return to full association with God's community a system of sacrifices was established. Such sacrificial services may strike us as being somewhat external to the inner dimensions of sin. The prophets thought so too; they were persuaded, therefore, that the nation of Israel would be replaced in time by a more spiritual kingdom and covenant – a community of faith!

We must emphasize the fact that Israel was created as a community. It was chosen to be "a kingdom of priests." That is to say, this nation, as an organized people, was designed to stand in a special relationship to God, both corporately and individually. As such it did not consist of an aggregate of individuals; also the interpersonal relationships within the national community were the object of God's redemptive intent. We must not overlook this aspect of God's activity in making a nation His very own.

God arranged a covenant with this people. This was, however, not the kind of contract over whose terms Israel might bargain with God. The word *berith*, used by our Hebrew text, stands for unilateral action on God's part. Now it may be of some interest at this point to digress for a moment to point out that one of the contributions archaeology has made to our understanding of the covenant relationship is the observation that the *form* of this covenant, as described in Ex. 20—24, is that of ancient Middle Eastern suzerainty covenants. That is to say, it follows the pattern used by kings of old in spelling out the terms of service for their subjects. It was customary for the monarch, first of all, to set forth what he had done for his people. Then he would outline in detail what he expected of his people. At this juncture his subjects were given the opportunity of accepting or rejecting the king's offer. After the subjects had agreed to accept the king's terms, the covenant was sealed by the sprinkling of blood from a sacrifice. Now if you will check the five chapters of Exodus just referred to, you will note that in offering Israel His very own *berith* God chose to use this familiar pattern.

By choosing Israel as His people, the Lord, of course, proceeded in judgment over other nations. As an holy nation, Israel was separated from other peoples. In fact this community of grace was given the responsibility of extending God's rule either by winning over or by exterminating other nations. We must always keep this side of Israel's task in mind as we read about what Gerhard von Rad calls the "holy wars" of the Old Testament. These battles were fought to manifest the nature of God's holiness as an aspect of God's will that brooks neither opposition nor defilement.

Israel as God's kingdom was shaped as a theocracy. The individual entered this kingdom by way of circumcision. If at any point he transgressed God's law, he could be reaccepted into the community by offering the prescribed sacrifices. Here is how God proposed to reestablish His rule among men. He hoped that other nations might see in Israel an example worth emulating. Israel, however, failed in her destiny. In time God's kingdom of priests clamored for a king of their own. They wanted to be like other nations. Instead of being different, separated from other peoples, Israel preferred to conform to the pattern of earthly kingdoms. Its representatives came to Samuel, therefore, with the request, "Now make us a king to judge us like all the nations." (1 Sam. 8:6)

You will recall that Samuel himself was deeply distressed by this request. He understood what was involved. Yet God Himself, in "divine forbearance" (Rom. 3:25), accepted this new situation. He ordered Samuel to provide a king for His people. To give the proper assurances to Samuel, God told him that this people had not rejected the prophet but rather God Himself. It remained a kingdom of priests, despite the fact that it now had a royal ruler of its own.

The external expansion of God's rule became an especially prominent feature of Israel in the time of David and of Solomon. In fact we will not go far wrong in saying that in its day and even later the kingdom of

David was understood to be synonymous with the rule of God. The idolatry of Solomon, however, shook the nation to its very foundations. Even without prophetic illumination it became obvious that God's rule and Solomon's kingdom were not at all coextensive.

The realization grew that the true kingdom of God would come only in the last days. Accordingly the concept of the kingdom took on more spiritual dimensions. The prophets began to speak of a remnant in Israel, a root from which a new plant would grow. They stressed the fact that God was about to do something new, such as bringing in the Gentiles to share in the grace of God. Whatever form the kingdom of God might take in the future they were sure it would not come without judgment upon Israel itself. In context the concept of the Suffering Servant began to occupy the thought of one of God's greatest prophets. Israel itself must experience the fires of God's wrath for its many iniquities; as a nation it had chosen to serve other gods. It must suffer the consequences of disobedience; but this very suffering would bring healing and salvation at the coming of *the* Suffering Servant, God's true prince.

The prophet Jeremiah, therefore, had already spoken of a new covenant that God would make with His people, saying (31:31-34): "Behold, the days are coming, says the Lord, when I will make a new covenant with the house of Israel and the house of Judah, not like the covenant which I made with their fathers when I took them by the hand to bring them out of the land of Egypt, My covenant which they broke, though I was their husband, says the Lord. But this is the covenant which

I will make with the house of Israel after those days, says the Lord: I will put My law within them, and I will write it upon their hearts; and I will be their God, and they shall be My people. And no longer shall each man teach his neighbor and each his brother, saying, 'Know the Lord,' for they shall all know Me, from the least of them to the greatest, says the Lord; for I will forgive their iniquity, and I will remember their sin no more." This new rule would be characterized by the forgiveness of sins, by fellowship with God, by the inwardness of God's law. Quite obviously such a covenant would be a creation of God's grace. Sin, rather than enemy nations, would come under judgment. This new community, where all would share fully in knowing God, would be an instrument of God's mercy, just as Israel of old had been called to be the vehicle for reestablishing God's rule over and among men. We shall do well to note how the same characteristics that had prevailed during the days of Israel's choice were to apply to the covenant of the future.

The prophets were sure that this new kingdom would outlast and prevail over the empires of this world. Daniel, for example, identified the stone of Nebuchadnezzar's dream as the kingdom which would destroy the powers represented by the various parts of a huge statue (ch. 2). This same prophet also described one "like the Son of man," to whom would be given dominion, glory, and rule (ch. 7). These are references to a kingdom that was to come, which was to supersede the external empires represented by the various beasts described in this very context.

Naturally the question arose, "When will this kingdom of God come?" There were those who answered the question in political terms, anticipating that God would raise up a scion from David's lineage, one who would drive out the hated Romans and establish Israel as a nation. Others were sure that this world was much too evil for the creation of the kingdom of heaven. They expected the coming of the heavenly Son of man, who would bring to an end the course of history itself and establish a new city of Zion as the center of God's rule. Still others maintained that if Israel would only keep the Law properly, just for one Sabbath, God's kingdom would come. A small group of Essenes even moved out into the desert of Judah, in keeping with their understanding of Is. 40, believing they were the true remnant and persuaded that their understanding of and loyalty to the Law would bring in the kingdom. But there were also a few people, individuals like Zechariah, Mary, Joseph, Simeon, Anna, and Joseph of Arimathaea, who were sure that God would act more radically than this. They awaited the kingdom of God, realizing that it would not come with commotion or observation, as was popularly supposed. These were given a true understanding of the words from Habakkuk (1:5): "Look among the nations, and see; wonder and be astounded. For I am doing a work in your days that you would not believe if told" (cf. Acts 13:41). In the meantime Israel's rabbis were teaching people that the Messianic age would come, and that righteousness would reign among men.

Into this kind of situation came John the Baptist and Jesus of Nazareth to proclaim that the kingdom of God had come (cf. Matt. 3:2 and Mark 1:15). The moment had come for God to proceed with the assumption of His royal rule. Men were to repent and accept this good news in faith.

Jesus Himself, the instrument of this rule, was severely tested in His obedience after His anointing by the Spirit. Satan tempted Him with the proposition that He ought rather to direct His attention to man's physical hunger and use His divine power to make bread. This would be one way of gathering a following, as the Caesars of Rome had discovered. Again, the devil proposed that Jesus use His supernatural power to attract the attention of people by something of a circus stunt, jumping from the pinnacle of the temple. Obviously this would have brought many people together out of sheer curiosity. The devil also suggested to Him that He might seize political power and so establish Himself as king. However, our Lord violently rejected all of these temptations. He had come as God's servant to suffer for men's sins and in that way inaugurate, establish, and extend that new covenant of which Jeremiah had spoken. His trials only made Him more certain and determined to carry out His task in keeping with the Father's will.

We must note that, in a very real sense, Jesus embodied this kingdom in His person. The rule of God which He manifested was marked by the same features as those we examined when we were discussing the Sinaitic covenant. Jesus, of course, came as an act of God's grace. He invaded our existence from beyond, so to speak. Men did not bring Him down from heaven nor up from the depths of the abyss (cf. Rom. 10:6, 7). He came by way of the Incarnation as God's own Son.

At His coming God Himself dwelt among men. Interestingly enough, the evangelist John puts it like this: "The Word became flesh and tabernacled among us" (John 1:14). Jesus in His person replaced and fulfilled the ancient institution of the wilderness tabernacle, the tent of God's presence. As God's Son, the true Israel, Jesus came to do God's will perfectly. "My food is to do the will of Him who sent Me," He once said (John 4:34). Therefore at His baptism the servant words of Isaiah 42 were applied to Him.

To create a new community Jesus first chose four, then twelve disciples. They were part of the faithful remnant in Israel. Departing from the practice of other teachers, He chose His disciples; they did not choose Him. Here He followed the divine pattern of choice in grace. His nation had forgotten this point. What this people was incapable of doing, He proposed to fulfill by His mission and His words. He came to be Himself obedient and to create a new kind of people, that might serve God from the heart.

He came as David's greater son, to accomplish what Solomon had failed to do. He became incarnate of David's line to erect the abiding temple of God, even though it meant the destruction of the sanctuary in Jerusalem. His work proceeded in judgment over Israel's own hardness of heart.

The kingdom of God came to men in the person of Jesus Christ. To make sure that His disciples would understand some of the dimensions of this event, He told a number of parables about the kingdom. Some of these we propose to cover in this study. Jesus had come as the scion of David's line. His disciples expected Him to assume His rule quickly and with power. He had to remind them that bringing the kingdom was like sowing seed. They must reckon with an interval of time before the day of the harvest, the moment when He would assume His rule in unobscured splendor and power. To this point we shall revert in particular when we take up the parable of the Seed Growing Secretly. (Mark 4:26-29)

Jesus chose twelve apostles to constitute the new Israel. On Pentecost day they and the community in which they served became the church, as God's last great redemptive act within history. There needed to be twelve apostles in the new Israel just as there had been twelve patriarchs in days of old. That is why Judas needed to be replaced by Matthias before Pentecost. For God proposed to do a new thing but along the pattern of the old.

Once more God acted in grace. He identified Himself with this small redeemed community in Jerusalem. Among this people He had chosen to dwell, neither in a tabernacle nor in a temple, but in Word and Sacrament. In this way His rule has come down to us; for the Gospel that we proclaim is the word of His kingdom. The church has been created to live out the new dimensions of a life marked by love, peace, patience, forgiveness, and suffering.

We are this community. Let us never forget it. In the Third Article of our Creed we call ourselves the "communion of saints." Hereby we remind ourselves that also the interpersonal relationships prevailing among us have been redeemed. The church is not just an aggregation of individuals. It is a fellowship in which each member has responsibilities toward his fellow members. One of the old church fathers used to say, "Unus Christianus, nullus Christianus."

As the church goes about her work of proclaiming the Gospel, God's rule proceeds not only in grace, but also in judgment over man's sins. It is not Amalekites and Moabites that face us. It is the hosts of hell, the world, and our own flesh that oppose God. These resist His rule; and so they come under God's judgment as the church goes about her task, until that moment when our Lord returns to create what we are accustomed to call the kingdom of glory.

The general features of this final phase in God's rule are provided in the Book of Revelation. The splendor of it all will become manifest at the moment of our Lord's return, which will, of course, be an act of God's grace. We shall not force Him from heaven by our performance. On the contrary, in His own good time He will appear as the Son of man in the clouds of heaven to dwell among us in unveiled glory. We are assured that then there will be no temple among men. No such edifice will be required; for God Himself will be the temple of this heavenly community. (Rev. 21:22)

The consummation of our hope is spoken of in terms of a new Jerusalem. There is no more emphatic way of underscoring the community aspects of our life in heaven. There we can expect to have God's will prevail fully. His mercy will have found its goal; nothing that is defiled or sinful can enter this kingdom. God's rule will have proceeded in final judgment over all that is in rebellion against Him. For that reason one of the characteristics of the kingdom as it appears in history will vanish. In the new Jerusalem there will be neither missionary opportunities nor responsibilities; for every one of God's elect, the 144,000, will be there.

We have dealt so extensively with the concept of the kingdom of God in order to remind ourselves that in the light of our considerations this is the central theme of our Scriptures. In our discussion of the parables we must constantly keep reminding ourselves that it is precisely this redemptive activity that Jesus had in mind as He told His parables. In fact when we read the words, "The kingdom of God is like . . . ," we might paraphrase them by saying, "When God is active redemptively in order to reestablish His rule over and among men, this work is like. . . ."

The rule of God is at work among us right here and now. The parables do not describe something that goes on in heaven. They were designed to tell us what goes on here, among men, when God is busy reestablishing Himself as our King. We are dealing with what Emil Brunner has called the "parabola of redemption." God's plan was devised in eternity, it sweeps through history and ends beyond history in the realm of everlasting life. God has been at work among us more. The Scriptures tell us of the events by which God chose to manifest Himself. These sweep through history and by the means of grace pick us up, as it were, to move us along through life in the company of God's redeemed toward that kingdom which will be marked by the undimmed splendor of God's abiding presence. The parables of Jesus tell us about this kingdom. As we study them, we ought never to lose sight of the divine thrust in the mystery revealed to us who have seen in Jesus Christ and His work the very heart of God's purposes for and with us.

THE AUTOMATIC ACTION OF THE SOIL
(Mark 4:26-29)

And He went on to say: With the kingdom of God it is as though a man would scatter the seed on the soil and go to sleep and get up night and day, and the seed would sprout and grow up without him knowing just how. The soil spontaneously bears fruit: first the blade, then the stalk, then the full grain in the stalk. Then, whenever the crop permits, he at once puts in the sickle because the harvest is at hand.

Preliminary Observations:

Mark alone has this parable, which describes the kingdom in terms of its origins and development. It belongs to what Jeremias calls a "collection of seed parables," gathered into one chapter by Mark — as he believes.

Grant (*Interpreter's Bible*, VII, p. 704) holds that this parable and the one of the Mustard Seed form a pair; one sets forth the secrecy and mystery of growth, and the other the astonishing contrast between small beginnings and universal achievement. Others hold that Matthew's Parable of the Tares is another version of this same parable. This is Juelicher's view (II, 545). But the only ground for this conjecture is that there are some verbal coincidences in the two accounts.

In fact the two parables differ widely in their details and in their point of comparison. It is most probable that the parables of the Sower, the Soil, and the Tares constituted an original trilogy told by our Lord in the setting described by Mark at the beginning of the chapter. Mark has preserved the first and second; Matthew has retained the first and the third; Luke gives us only the first one. (Cf. Swete, *Parables of the Kingdom*, p. 17)

In the main we can detect four general ways in which this parable has been interpreted in the past:
- a) There are those who hold that the theme is the divine seed which Christ implants in the heart and in the church;
- b) In the 19th century it was generally interpreted to describe the gradual evolution of the kingdom in human society;
- c) The eschatological interpretation, with the picture of the harvest signifying the speedy in-breaking of the kingdom;
- d) The view of "realized eschatology": that the parable is related to the immediate crisis brought on by the coming of Jesus.

All of these have some element of truth in them. It will be our task to unfold the meaning of this parable in the light of the concept of the kingdom as we have tried to analyze it.

Textual Matters:

The parable begins with what Jeremias (p. 11) calls "one of Mark's typical link-phrases." It is found also at 2:27; 4:2, 21, 24; 6:10; 7:9; 8:21; 9:1. The imperfect of the verb would seem to suggest that this is intended to be part of the discourse given to the crowd from the boat. This would mean that this parable is given as part of the "much teaching" mentioned in v. 2.

The comparison established by οὕτως — ὡς is not limited to one point of the parable but includes the whole statement, from the sprouting of the seed to the harvest. It is a kind of dative beginning, of which there are two other instances in Mark, namely, at 4:31 and 13:34. Jeremias (p. 78) suggests that an underlying Aramaic *le* is echoed here. Therefore it should not be translated, "It is like," but with, "It is the case with . . . as with. . . ."

Dodd (p. 180) lists three interpretations of this parable as exclusive of each other. He points out that some take the kingdom to be like the seed; others like the whole process of growth; still others like the harvest. But these three can really all be brought into one statement, as Wohlenberg (Zahn) does when he gives this parable the title: "Die von selbst der Ernte entgegenwachsende Saat."

The article is used with σπόρος, because the seed has already been mentioned. The reason for the subjunctive of the aorist βάλῃ may be that it points back to what had been said in the parable of the Sower.

The Nestle text does not have ἐάν after ὡς. But the particle seems necessary according to all rules of Greek grammar. It was easily lost in copying; the next word begins with the same letters.

V. 27. The subjunctive form καθεύδῃ and the others are probably so by attraction and are meant in the sense of present indicatives, which make the narrative more vivid. Mark, you know, was a man who could not help telling a story interestingly.

ὡς has sometimes been taken in a temporal sense. It is probably better to think of it as expressing manner.

It was Erasmus who first suggested that the αὐτός might refer to the seed rather than to the "man." In that case it might mean that the seed grows without reflection or concentration on its own part.

μηκύνηται is middle. This stresses the internal power for growing up. It is part of the mystery of growth.

V. 28. The Septuagint uses the word αὐτομάτη (Lev. 25:5, 11) of the seed growing up, without new planting, during the sabbatical and jubilee years. The word is also used in Acts 12:10 of a gate opening for Peter "of itself." Classical Greek often uses the same term to describe the bringing forth of the earth in the golden age.

The verb καρποφορεῖ is used here of the incipient stages of the fruit-bearing plant.

The adjective πλήρης is an unchangeable one. There is no need of putting σῖτος into the accusative. The nominative puts special emphasis on the grain, which is the end and aim of the seed growing spontaneously.

V. 29. The expression παραδοῖ presents certain difficulties. Some suggest that it is used as in 1 Peter 2:23, where it is said that Jesus *surrendered* (yielded) His cause to Him who judges aright. Most modern commentators, however, accept the meaning "allow," "permit." The verb is here in the subjunctive.

The harvest is an ancient and familiar symbol for the end of all things, the day of the Lord. ἀποστέλλει τὸ δρέπανον is an echo of Joel 3:13 (LXX).

The verb παρέστηκεν also occurs in Joel 3:13, the prophet's description of the day of Jehovah.

Exegetical Items:

The parable of the Sower occurs before our present text. The latter is sometimes called (KJV) the parable of the Seed Growing Secretly. From the explanation of the parable of the Sower it is clear that the seed is the Word, the message of the kingdom. The purpose of that parable was to show what happens when the Word of the kingdom is proclaimed among men.

The present parable of the Soil (Oesterley) also deals with the "mystery of the kingdom." It relates to the Sower by virtue of the fact that it describes how the Word grows in the fourth group of people, represented by the good soil. By the sowing of the seed the kingdom is brought to these hearts; and our present parable intends to describe the development of that seed until it reaches the time of harvest.

We must note, however, that there is a passage between the two parables mentioned. It covers vv. 21 to 23 and is a statement on the subject of Jesus Himself, as the Light, having come into the world to be made manifest, not to remain hidden. If we recall, in this connection, that Mark is the Gospel of the Son of man, then we begin to realize that the parable of the Soil was told to show how this unveiling of Jesus as the Son of man was to take place: by sowing the Word until it reaches the moment of harvest.

Jesus had come as David's great Son, in whom the promises once given to that ancient king were fulfilled. His kingdom would have no end. For a time people believed that this promise referred to Solomon; but they had been disillusioned. That kingdom was not God's rule. This became evident with the idolatry of Solomon's later years. Now the great Heir had come. But how was He to establish an everlasting rule? That is the point of the parable. This Son of David would assume His rule by the proclamation of the Word. This, like seed, would grow in the soil of men's affairs until such time as the harvest would be ready and the Son of man would assume His power in full and unobscured splendor.

Dodd interprets the time of sowing as the period of the prophets and the harvest as "the day of the Son of man" (p. 180), that is, the time of the first advent. This is in keeping with his basic concept of "realized eschatology," his view that the point of the parables applies only to the years of Jesus' earthly ministry. The verb tenses, however, and particularly their subjunctive mood, as used in the parable, would seem to preclude this interpretation. The parable was told to reveal what had just begun, now that the kingdom of God was at hand in the person of Jesus.

The Jews spoke of taking on the yoke of the "malkuth." This was done by saying the "shemah" daily.

They took on the yoke by submitting themselves to the Law (cf. Dalman, *Worte Jesu*, pp. 79, 80). By keeping every jot and tittle of the Law they sought to compel the coming of the kingdom (*Interpreter's Bible* VII, 146). They sought to do so "by a system of conduct refined and methodically regulated to the last detail, a regime which as such was a work of one's own decision, will, doing, and capability" (Otto, *Son of Man*, p. 120). The Zealots even went so far as to believe that open revolt would force the hand of God.

Jesus used this parable to correct some of these false notions, some of which His disciples may have absorbed in their previous training. He stresses, therefore, the spontaneity of growth. The kingdom is self-developing. It grows on itself and is not brought in by the efforts of men. (Luther: "Non propriis viribus, meritis, aut operibus.")

The good seed scattered by the divine Sower no longer requires His visible presence. He dwells in His Word. Inherent in it are the powers of growth. At harvest time, however, He will return. "Jesus Christ manifested His visible presence and personal intervention in the foundation of His kingdom, but will do so no more until it is consummated on earth; this kingdom, meanwhile, by its inherent driving power will spontaneously grow and develop until the end of time" (Fonck, p. 118). In the meantime the powers of the kingdom are at work in the church as she sows the word. You and I, therefore, share in the task of extending God's rule, not by weapons of destruction as in the instance of ancient Israel, but by the proclamation of the Gospel.

The kingdom of God is a power even now at work in the world (Luke 10:9-11). When the seed was originally sown by our Lord, forces were set in motion which one day will produce a full harvest of people who serve God "in righteousness and blessedness." The kingdom has a goal: the absolute and unchallenged reign of God over His people in eternal splendor. (Cf. 1 Cor. 15:27.)

The harvest time is the "Last Day" (Joel 3:13; Rev. 14:15). For all who have come under God's reign, it will be a day of deliverance. Then sin and evil will no longer frustrate God's rule; sin and disease will no longer afflict His people. On that day the tyranny of Satan will be completely crushed. Every knee will bow before His name and every tongue confess that Jesus Christ is Lord to the glory of God the Father (Phil. 2:10, 11). Jesus here implies that the time will come when God's kingdom will have accomplished its purpose in history. Every day is carrying us forward to that goal, though no man, not even the great Son of man, knows when it will be reached. It rests with the Great Sower who is also the Reaper. With Him there is no real delay, no premature ingathering: "whenever the crop permits, he at once puts in the sickle because the harvest is at hand."

The day of harvest will not bring the reestablishment of Israel. The disciples were wrong in asking, on the day of the Ascension, "Lord, will you at this time restore the kingdom to Israel?" (Acts 1:6). They did not yet fully understand the point of the present parable: the invasion of history by the Word of God's kingdom growing like seed until the time of harvest.

Homiletical Suggestion:

The central truth of the parable of the Automatic Action of the Soil might be put as follows: Since God's redemptive activity resembles the process of growth, let us accept God's method of working, without ourselves becoming disillusioned; for growth is spontaneous, gradual, and purposeful (teleological).

The malady to which we might, therefore, address ourselves in the homiletical treatment of this parable could well be the tendency to become disappointed with life in the church.

Introductory: Our God is the Lord of the universe and of history. Therefore we speak of His kingdom of power. But this is not what we pray for when we say, "Thy kingdom come." In His grace God identifies Himself with His redeemed community, His church. But life in this community has its shortcomings and its disappointments. When will God take His power and strike with His strong right arm? We can hardly avoid raising this question.

GOD AT WORK AMONG US

I. He Works Creatively.
   A. The seed of the Word: the proclamation of what He has done and will do for man's salvation.
   B. The soil: the hearts of those people, that group, where the Word grows.
   C. Growth is spontaneous.

II. God's Power Unfolds Gradually.
   A. This truth is sobering,

    B. It is realistic,
    C. It is comforting.
III. God Works with His Own Ends in View.
    A. The harvest is the end of time;
    B. We live even now in the eschatological dimension, knowing the final outcome of God's activity.

Conclusion: Let us not be deceived by appearances or misled by false standards of success. It is *God's* kingdom we proclaim. We already live under *His* rule.

THE TWO SONS
(Matthew 21:28-32)

Now, what do you think? A man had two sons. He approached the first one and said, "Son, go and work in my vineyard today." He said, "I go, Sir!" But he did not go. Then he went to the second one with the same request. But he answered, "I'm not going to." Later, however, he changed his mind and went. Which of the two did the will of the father? They say, "The latter." Jesus says to them, "Of a truth I tell you that the publicans and harlots precede you into the kingdom of God. For John came to you in the way of righteousness, but you did not believe in him. The tax collectors and harlots, however, did believe in him. When you saw this, you did not even then change your minds and believe him."

Textual Matters:

The chief textual problem is that of the order of the two sons. We have given the order as it occurs in the Nestle text. Both the KJV and the RSV reverse this sequence. In his apparatus Nestle indicates that the latter might well be the right one. The necessary changes in v. 31 have to be taken into account.

Some texts offer a third possibility. They reverse the order but do not make an alteration in v. 31. This would mean that those whom Jesus asked were determined to keep Him from being right.

The Nestle order seems to fit the situation best. The parable follows the incident of cursing the fig tree and the question of the Messiah's authority. It is followed by the parable of the Wicked Husbandmen. These are all items that deal with the relationship of the religious leaders in Jerusalem to Jesus as the Messiah.

Exegetical Items:

The figure of the vineyard is familiar to us. In the fifth chapter of Isaiah it represents the people of Israel. It is a symbol of Israel as God's very own possession, His *segullah* (Ex. 19:5).

Sonship is a concept to depict the covenant relationship of Israel with God. Moses was instructed to say to Pharaoh: "Thus says the Lord, 'Israel is My firstborn son and I say to you "Let My son go that he may serve Me." ' " (Ex. 4:22, 23)

As a covenant people, Israel was called to serve God in righteousness. However, as Isaiah put it: "He looked for justice, but behold, bloodshed; for righteousness, but behold, a cry" (5:7). In the days of Jesus religious affairs were the specific responsibility of the Sanhedrin, consisting of Sadducees, Pharisees, and lay persons known as elders of the people. These looked with disdain on ordinary folk known as "people of the soil" *('am haaretz)*. Harlots and tax collectors in particular were objects of reproach. The latter often worked on the Sabbath; they represented political oppression and sometimes foreign domination. Harlots, of course, lived in immorality. There was hope for neither in Judaism.

Yet when John the Baptist came, preaching "the way of righteousness," as it is stated here, it was not the religious elite that listened to him. They did not recognize his coming as God breaking in to do a new thing, to create a new people. Publicans and harlots, however, did — and that in great number.

Jeremiah had spoken of the new covenant as a time of forgiveness. This was to be God's "way of righteousness." John, therefore, quoted from Isaiah 40 to depict God's approach in terms of a highway for the King. Etymologically, you see, the Hebrew *zedakah* ("righteousness") means "smoothness." In fact to this day Arabs use this term with reference to roads. In righteousness God had determined to smooth out the way between Himself and Israel, offering forgiveness. John proclaimed the forgiveness of sins and repentance. His baptism was another Red Sea act of God's creating and liberating a people for Himself.

John called Israel to repentance. This scandalized the members of the Sanhedrin. For were they not God's son? Had not God made a special covenant with this people? John called Israel to repentance because Judaism, in distinction from the religion of the Old Testament, described Israel's acceptance of the covenant as a meritorious act. There was an old Jewish parable, for example, which told the story of God offering a field (the Torah) to all the nations. None, however, wanted the responsibility to cultivate this field except Israel. (Cf. Strack-Billerbeck, I:865.)

There was another tradition, one which is worth knowing about, because it helps us to understand the story of Pentecost as given in Acts 2. According to this view, on the 50th day after Israel had left Egypt, God had offered His Law at Sinai to all the nations of the earth, to each of the 70 in its respective language. He offered it to the Moabites. They wanted to know its terms. God read the Law; but when He reached the sixth commandment, they replied, "Thank you very much; we were born in adultery." Then God proposed to give His Law to the descendants of Esau, but they would not accept the prohibition on killing. The Edomites likewise declined on the principle that stealing had been part of their inherited way of life. Only Israel promised to obey. The Jews were quite proud of the fact that they had made this choice. The Sanhedrin, some of whose members were engaged in a running argument with Jesus, epitomized this feeling of special privilege. They headed a people which had promised to obey; but, like the son in the parable, they really did not follow through on their promise. They refused to accept God on His terms, especially not on the basis of forgiveness and repentance. Their reaction to John's preaching provided the evidence that they were in fact disobedient.

Harlots and tax collectors had responded otherwise. Many of them were delighted to accept the offer of forgiveness. They realized only too well that they were wretched sinners. They were received into God's kingdom, for it had come for sinners only. Even then the religious leaders in Jerusalem did not change their minds. They would not accept the "way of righteousness" as God's offer of communion on the basis of being forgiven.

The parable itself ends at v. 30. It is very brief. Vv. 31 and 32 provide the setting and the explanation. By replying to the question of Jesus, "Which of the two did the will of his father?" the members of the Sanhedrin were confronted directly by the challenge of the parable, the claim of Jesus as embodying God's "way of righteousness" (cf. Rom. 1:16, 17). They rejected the invitation inherent in the parable; so tax gatherers and publicans, people deemed to be outside the commonwealth of Israel, entered the kingdom ahead and often to the exclusion of those who thought of themselves as already being in the kingdom by virtue of their being Jews.

The importance of this little parable for an understanding of the nature of God's kingdom can hardly be overstated. God is determined to reestablish His rule among men by forgiving their sins. Obedience consists in the response of faith, of accepting this offer of a new covenant, not like the one made with Israel, when God led that people out of Egypt.

Homiletical Suggestions:

Introductory: God has always retained the initiative in dealing with men as His creatures. He has been their Redeemer, breaking into history, promising Abraham an inheritance and offering Israel a covenant. Later He became incarnate to confront men with His gracious will to forgive their iniquities and to remember their sin no more. That chapter began with the preaching of John the Baptist. His emphasis on repentance and forgiveness made it clear that God's kingdom had come —

FOR SINNERS ONLY

I. Israel, the First Son
   A. Promised obedience;
   B. Perverted God's grace by viewing acceptance as a meritorious achievement;
   C. Religious leaders in Jerusalem, therefore, excluded from kingdom;
   D. Exclusion of all those who attempt to create the terms of sonship.

II. Sinners Represented by the Second Son
   A. God's "way of righteousness" means His offer of forgiveness,
   B. Repentance and faith as acceptance of this offer,
   C. Entrance into the kingdom by faith.

Conclusion: The church proclaims the Word of the kingdom as God's offer of forgiveness. Baptism brings men into this community of forgiveness. The Lord's Supper is the "visible word" of forgiveness. All this is intended for sinners only.

THE BARREN FIG TREE
(Luke 13:6-9)

Then He told the following parable: A certain man owned a fig tree which he had planted in his vineyard; and he came looking for fruit on it, but found none. So he said to the caretaker, "Look, three years have passed since I came looking for fruit on this fig tree and found none. Cut it down; just why does it keep on wasting the ground?" But he, the caretaker, said to him by way of reply: "Sir, leave it this year yet, while I spade around it and throw fertilizer around it. Then, if it produces, leave it for the future! But if it does not, you shall cut it down."

Textual Matters:

V. 6. The δέ connects the parable with what has gone before. It suggests that the story of the fig tree is illustrative of the point made previously in the matter of repentance.

The word for "fig tree" (συκῆ) occupies an emphatic position in the sentence, even though fig trees were not the most important plants in a Palestinian vineyard. The *Expositor's Greek Testament* says that the fig tree was chosen "by way of protest against assumed inalienable privilege" on the part of Israel. We shall see later that this fig tree is probably a symbol of the city of Jerusalem rather than of Israel as a whole. Such a tree was one of the most common trees in Palestine. The tree of the parable had been planted, and the owner was enjoying its growth.

Vineyards were frequently located on hillsides or on peaks (Is. 5:1), which were terraced whenever necessary. Every such vineyard was surrounded by a hedge or a stone wall to keep out destructive animals (Num. 22:24; Ps. 80:8-13; Prov. 24:31; Is. 5:5). The ground was cleared of stones, the vines were planted, a booth or tower was erected for the watchman, a press was constructed, and a vat was hewn in the rock (Is. 5:1-7; Matt. 21:33-41). Laborers were sometimes hired to work in it (Matt. 20: 1-16), for it was necessary to prune the vines, dig about them, and keep the ground free of weeds (Lev. 25:3; Prov. 24:30, 31; Is. 5:6; John 15:2). The vines were allowed to spread on the ground, the stock not being supported, only the fruit-bearing branches being slightly raised from the earth. (Is. 16:8; Ezek. 17:6)

V. 7: "Three years," that is, from the time the tree ought to have begun bearing fruit, and not from the time of its planting. A tree hardly began bearing fruit until two or three years after its planting; then it bore two or three times a year.

ἔρχομαι, a progressive present: "It is three years from the time when I keep coming."

ἔκκοψον, a sign of impatience: "Cut it out from the roots! Dig it up!" Cf. Luke 3:9 for the figure of the axe already being laid at the root of the tree.

καί gives an additional reason. "Why, in addition to doing no good, does it sterilize the ground?"

V. 9: εἰς τὸ μέλλον appears after the second conditional clause in some manuscripts. In most of them these words are given before the condition. Zahn (p. 527, note 82) refers to the position before the conditional clause as seemingly being of Egyptian origin and says that most of the Greek manuscripts and all the Latin ones give the phrase after the second conditional statement.

The expression εἰς τὸ μέλλον is used in Greek for "the coming year," "next year" (Plutarch, especially). In 1 Tim. 6:19 it means simply "for the future." It seems to fit best after the first conditional clause. Under any circumstances we must reckon with an ellipsis, probably εὖ ἔχει (EGT) or καλῶς ἔχει (Zahn).

Exegetical Items:

There can be no doubt that the parable of the Fig Tree was spoken to the crowds in Jerusalem after certain individuals had brought the news of the people killed in the temple by order of Pilate. Those who told Him of the incident must have hinted that such a calamity must be evidence that the people who had been murdered were guilty of some special sin. To their report of an execution, Jesus Himself added the incident of the 18 people killed by the falling of the tower of Siloam.

As Thornton Wilder's *The Bridge of San Luis Rey* reminds us, such calamities naturally pose the question, Why? The Jews of that day, as well as people today, often attributed some extraordinary degree of guilt to such as were killed in the manner described here. To this common misconception Jesus replied with the words, "Not at all; but unless you repent, you shall all likewise perish." The implication is clear: We are all guilty of punishment and so deserve to perish. God, however, deals graciously with men by not permitting destruction to overtake them.

The answer of Jesus to the news of tragedy contains the further suggestion that the preaching of John concerning repentance (Luke 3:1 ff.; 7:29), and its continuation by Jesus (5:32 and 11:32), had gone unheeded especially in Jerusalem. There was still time to repent. The parable, therefore, was addressed to God's own city both as a warning and as an invitation to turn to God while there was still time.

In the accounts of Matthew and Mark the story of the cursing of the fig tree (Matt. 21:18-22; Mark 11:12-14) serves as a counterpart to this parable found in Luke. The action of Jesus on that Monday of Holy Week was symbolic of the same truth expressed by the present parable; i. e., the barren fig tree stood for the attitude of Jerusalem toward the preaching of John the Baptist and of Jesus.

The key to the understanding of the present parable is the interpretation of the planting of the fig tree in the vineyard of a "certain man." The vineyard is, of course, a picture of the people of Israel. Is. 5:7: "For the vineyard of the Lord of hosts is the house of Israel. . . ." This figure is repeated often in the Old Testament. (Cf. Is. 27:2-6; Jer. 12:10)

It has been suggested that the fig tree is to be considered as practically synonymous with the vineyard; in other words, that the fig tree represents all of Israel. The "Hirschberger Bibel," for example, says, "Hier bedeutet wohl der Feigenbaum hauptsaechlich die juedische Kirche, welche keine Fruechte des Glaubens brachte, der Weinberg aber das ganze Land, in welchem die Kirche gepflanzet wesen." This suggestion is naturally not unbiblical. However, the parable concentrates on a fig tree in the vineyard and not upon the vineyard itself. It might, of course, be urged that this is due to the loose construction of the parables. Such loosely knit parts, however, occur in the details of a parable rather than in the chief character.

In this connection it should be remembered that in Is. 1:8 Zion is spoken of as "a cottage in a vineyard." In other words, part of a vineyard is made the basis for a comparison with part of Israel. That might well be the case here. The fig tree, we believe, stands for Jerusalem. This is supported by the observation that in Is. 5:7 the men of Judah are called God's "pleasant plant."

This view receives further support by the fact that Jesus had just made special mention of Jerusalem (v. 4). Again, in v. 22 Luke notes that Jesus was journeying "toward Jerusalem" at this time. Moreover, the chapter closes with Jesus' lament over Jerusalem specifically. (Vv. 33-35)

If it is true that the fig tree stands for Jerusalem as part of the vineyard of Israel, then what are the three years spoken of by the owner of the vineyard? It is understood that units of time as such mean little in the counsels of Almighty God, who is represented by the owner of the vineyard. On the other hand, the reader is certainly inclined to look for some correspondence between the three-year period on the one hand and the single year on the other. Some commentators have suggested that the three years stand for the whole time from Abraham to Jesus, or even the whole history of the world before Christ (Theodor of Mopsuestia). Augustine understood them as representing three different dispensations: the era of natural law, of the Torah, and of grace. Theophylact identified the years with the ages of Moses, the prophets, and Jesus respectively. Still others (Olshausen, Luther) have taken the three years to refer to the actual calendar years of Christ's activity.

Grotius already took issue with this last interpretation, pointing out that, if these three years are to be taken in strict chronology, then the one year of additional grace must also be so understood. But this would create great difficulties; for, in point of fact, the season of additional and increased grace for Jerusalem lasted 40 years. It may be best, therefore, to interpret the three years as signifying the whole period of time from the establishment of Jerusalem as David's city. The extra year of probation then would represent the time during which Jerusalem served as the headquarters and center of the Christian church.

Without a doubt, the vinedresser in the parable represents Jesus. "How often would I have gathered thy children together," He lamented at the end of the chapter. No doubt, He often interceded with His Father for this people. Even on the cross He pleaded, "Father, forgive them; for they know not what they do." The door of repentance still remained open.

The ancient Greeks had a saying to the effect that the "feet of the avenging gods are wrapped in wool." The true God, however, warns his people very plainly of coming disaster unless they repent. "This is peculiar to the clemency of God," says St. Basil to the command, "'Cut it down!' that He does not bring in punishment silently or secretly; but by His threatenings first proclaims them to be at hand, thus inviting sinners to repentance." First the axe is laid to the root, as it was at the time of John the Baptist; later the tree is cut down.

It is interesting to note that the narrative of the parable was not finished. It is not stated whether the digging and dunging helped, or whether the tree still brought forth no fruit. In that way the parable was an invitation to the hearers to repent and bring forth fruit. Of Jerusalem we know that it brought forth no fruit. However, the time for its extinction came later. As yet there was time to change; hence the Lord did not reveal the ultimate fate of the fig tree.

In this parable the longsuffering of God and His wrath are balanced with each other as at no other place in the Bible. There is a mysterious line between the two. And so it may rightly be said that time is a factor in God's dealings with men although with God there really is no time.

This parable is not specifically introduced by the evangelist as a parable of the kingdom; yet it illustrates one of the great truths of the kingdom of God: His love and righteousness at work in the affairs of men in the interest of their repentance and subsequent salvation.

Homiletical Suggestions:

Introductory: God's kingdom is His saving will with men. The gate to salvation is repentance, which the Baptist came to preach and Jesus continued to proclaim in order to establish the kingdom.

The effect and the results of His work, however, were meager when compared with the significance of His message. His appeal for repentance went unheeded by most of His contemporaries.

The parable of the Fig Tree is one more urgent plea for repentance to escape destruction. It reveals the longsuffering of God and also His ultimate wrath over impenitent sinners. Its emphasis is on an additional season of grace for us. It speaks to us of

OUR YEAR OF PROBATION

I. Its Opportunities
    A. This is a time of *continued* grace
        1. In the parable the season of planting the fig tree and watching it grow until the time it is to bring forth fruit is a token of grace.
           a. The fig tree a very common tree;
           b. Yet planted in a choice place.
        2. This represents the choice of Jerusalem as "His pleasant plant" and of Jerusalem as the capital of this kingdom. (Is. 5:7) (1 Kings 2:36)
        3. Included are also the three years during which

the owner came repeatedly looking for fruit, which corresponds, in the case of Jerusalem, to the time from the creation of this city as God's own to the moment when Jesus spoke this parable. During these years the grace of God was showered upon Jerusalem in continuing measure.

Application: To us of the present, chosen out from the rest of the world, God's grace has been revealed in abiding measure. (Lutheran Church)

    B. This is a period of *increased* grace. In the parable of the fig tree the vinedresser asks for more time to treat the tree in a very special way; this corresponds to the increased grace revealed to Jerusalem during the later part of Jesus' ministry and especially during years of apostolic activity.

Application: We of today, in the midst of our year of probation, have experienced a special measure of God's grace.

        1. Printed Scriptures
        2. Radio and TV
        3. A land of freedom and wealth

II. Its Purpose
    A. Not to continue to bring forth no fruit, but to change and yield fruit in abundance;
    B. This corresponds to the purpose of Jesus' later ministry and of the apostolic ministry to bring His people to repentance and salvation.

Application: God's grace showered upon us to lead us to repentance.

III. Its Results
   A. The narrative of the parable is not concluded. If the tree changed, it remained in the vineyard.
   B. The case of Nineveh at the time of Jonah exemplifies this alternative.
   C. If the tree brought forth no fruit, it was cut out.
   D. Jerusalem itself a case in point. (Jesus cursing the fig tree on Monday of Holy Week was symbolic of the destruction to come upon this city.)
   E. Our year of probation is drawing to a close.

Conclusion: "Bring forth therefore fruits worthy of repentance!" Matt. 3:8. We are now living in our YEAR OF PROBATION. *Now* is the acceptable year of the Lord; now is the day of salvation. "Today, if ye shall hear His voice, harden not your hearts" (Heb. 3:7, 8). "Thy kingdom come!"

THE UNJUST JUDGE
(Luke 18:1-8)

Then He told them a parable to show that they ought to pray persistently and not to give up, saying: There was in a certain city a judge who neither feared God nor respected men; and there was a widow in that city. And she kept coming to him, saying, "Protect me against my enemy!" Now, for a time he did not want to. But later on he said within himself, "Even if I do not fear God nor respect men, still because this widow annoys me, I shall take up her defense, lest she finally come and cause me embarrassment." And the Lord said, "Listen to what the unjust judge says! Now, will not God avenge His elect who call to Him day and night — even though He delays long for them? I tell you He will come to their defense quickly. Yet when the Son of man comes — will He find faith on the earth?"

Textual Matters:

V. 1: δέ is a mild indication that what follows is connected with the discussion of the *parousia* in the previous chapter. The content of vv. 7 and 8 shows this still more clearly.

πρός: basic meaning "face to face." Here it might be translated, "Looking toward the need for persistent prayer."

V. 3: ἤρχετο is certainly used in an iterative sense.

The imperfect ἤθελεν in the next verse also indicates that this narrative is meant as a description of repeated action.

V. 4: ἐπὶ χρόνον: Vulgate: "per multum tempus," which is probably a little strong but indicates the direction: "for a considerable time."

ἐν ἑαυτῷ: It has been pointed out repeatedly that the characters in Luke's parables are given to talking to themselves; cf. parables of the Prodigal Son and of the Unjust Steward.

εἰς τέλος: There is a difference of opinion as to the interpretation of this phrase: "perpetuo, indesinenter" (Grotius; Kypke); "tandem," or even "omnino." There is an equal difference of opinion as to the position of this phrase: whether it goes with ἐρχομένη or with ὑπωπιάζῃ. The best solution seems to be that of taking the phrase in the meaning of "tandem" (finally; in the end) and to take it with the main verb of the sentence, ὑπωπιάζῃ, which Stoeckhardt, incidentally, takes very literally. (Cf. 1 Cor. 9:27.)

V. 6: "The judge of unrighteousness" is a Semitic construction which is equivalent to an adjectival construction: "the unjust judge." Significantly, his lovelessness toward fellow human beings is called "unrighteousness." It can be shown that the word "righteousness" has as one of its meanings love and consideration of the neighbor. (Cf. Titus 1:8.)

V. 7: μακροθυμεῖ "to be leisurely"; "to delay"; "to be patient"; "to be long-suffering." With καί we confront a difficulty in construction. The καί might reflect an Aramaic *waw* concessive, meaning "although." Jeremias

(p. 116) suggests that it could signify "who." In that instance the question could be translated: "Will not God give judgment in favor of His elect, He who listens to them patiently when they cry to Him day and night?" We have chosen the concessive meaning, mostly because the delay of the *parousia* seems to be the burden of the total context.

ἐκλεκτοί is one of the mighty words of Scripture, being the Old Testament *bachar,* a word used of God's action in choosing Israel as His covenant people (cf. Deut. 7: 7, 8). It is a kingdom term.

V. 8: ἐν τάχει. This expression means "right soon," but from any point of departure. Here it no doubt means that when the time of the second Advent has finally come, the execution of God's judgment will be sudden. The same idea is given in v. 24 of the previous chapter.

Exegetical Items:

This parable of the Unjust Judge is a companion to the story of the Selfish Neighbor (Luke 11:5-9). Both emphasize the need for *perseverance* in prayer, with this difference, however, that the latter stresses the need of persistent prayer in general while the present parable speaks of that need with particular reference to the second coming of the Lord.

For it is clear from the content of vv. 7 and 8 that this parable is told in connection with the description of the Last Day given toward the close of the previous chapter. Conforming to the request uttered by the parable, the church from the beginning has prayed for the second Advent. (Cf. Maranatha!, 1 Cor. 16:22.)

The point of comparison in this parable, then, is the effectiveness of persistency in prayer, and certainly not any similarity between the character of the judge and the nature of God. On this score there is only contrast. That seems to be the import of the juxtaposition of "judge of unrighteousness" and "God" (at the end of v. 6 and the beginning of v. 7, respectively). Paraphrasing these two sentences, the meaning seems to be, "If that unjust judge was finally moved to action against the widow's adversary, then certainly God, who is love and righteousness, will act to avenge His people at the Last Day."

Naturally a contrast can serve as a *tertium comparationis*, too. There is a note of similarity in this that both the judge and God act to avenge their clients. But that is only incidental.

It has been suggested that the widow of the parable is more than the "popular symbol of defenselessness" (Barnett) (cf. Ecclus. 35:14-19). Zahn raises the question whether there might not be an intended comparison between the loneliness of the widow and the state of the church here upon earth. The Scriptures speak at times of the widowhood of the church (Gal. 4:27) and of the people of God (Is. 54:4-7). Furthermore, final reception in glory is depicted as a marriage feast with Christ, the bridegroom (cf. Luke 5:35; John 3:29; Matt. 22:1 ff.; 25:1-13; 2 Cor. 11:2; Eph. 5:25-32; Rev. 19:7, 9; 21:2, 9).

This parable, no doubt, was intended to prepare the disciples and the Christians in general for what would seem to them a long delay of the final judgment. By a process called "prophetic foreshortening" (Dodd) the prophets of old, and even John the Baptist, spoke of the Messiah's coming in judgment as being simultaneous with His advent for salvation. There was no particular distinction between these two events in the prophets' eyes. They were right, of course, in a way. However, they left the impression — and Jesus Himself did, for very good reasons! — that the final "Day of the Lord" would come shortly, according to human calculations. The apostles were sure that Christ would return in their generation; and it was good they thought so. They were to watch and pray.

In this parable Jesus prepares His children for an *apparent* delay in the consummation of all things by judgment upon the enemies of the Lord. In the very first verse of the chapter the need for continuing in prayer is stressed, not only to keep the thought of the Last Day in the minds of the believers but especially to preserve men from the delusion, mentioned in 2 Peter 3, that since there was no essential change at all in the course of events (cf. Luke 17) the Day of Judgment would never come.

For them all, the words ἐν τάχει were to serve as a warning that when the Last Day would come, the execution of its events would follow at once. (Luke 17:24 — with the speed of lightning!)

The construction of v. 7 has afforded great difficulties to all interpreters. Some have gone to the length of omitting the words after καί, and changing the latter to ναί, as if in answer to the previous question, which, however, is rhetorical in every sense.

Others have taken the whole verse as one question and suggested that the καί is adversative, as in Hebrew. These same interpreters have taken μακροθυμεῖν in the sense of delaying, which it can have and certainly does in the book of Jesus Sirach [Ecclus.] 35:19 (ed. Rahlfs): καὶ ὁ κύριος οὐ μὴ βραδύνῃ οὐδὲ μὴ μακροθυμήσῃ ἐπ' αὐτοῖς. That makes good sense, reading, "Now, will God not avenge . . . although (while) He delays in their case." However, μακροθυμεῖν does not usually have this meaning; nor does one expect to find a Hebraistic construction of this kind in the Gospel of Luke.

Hofmann, therefore, suggested another solution (which Zahn follows). He pointed out that the strong rhetorical question is the equivalent in sense to an emphatic declarative sentence, and that the phrase beginning with καί is a continuation of such a positive statement implied by the previous question. In that case the meaning would be: God delays, indeed, but out of mercy and long-suffering with His elect; cf. 2 Peter 3:8, 9. This is probably reading a little more into the verse than the situation in the text either suggests or requires.

The first part of the verse points out that God will assuredly avenge His people who pray to Him day and night; and He will do so suddenly, when the time comes. The second part then adds the observation that it looks as though God were delaying.

"Yet will the Son of man find faith on earth when He comes?" Certainly He Himself knew that there would be a remnant of believers at the time of His second advent. The question, which sounds rather strange at first blush, is intended to keep the thought of faith before the eyes of the disciples and to urge them on to greater faith and perseverance in prayer. At the same time it is meant to show His followers that the duty of keeping faith alive on earth until His return was theirs. The last question, then, reemphasizes the need for persistency.

Introductory: For centuries the church has been praying, "Thy kingdom come!" Yet that kingdom has not come in glory. This situation might suggest that we take this matter less seriously. Jesus anticipated us. This parable was told to persuade us to persist.

PERSIST OR PERISH

I. Our Need
   A. We are beset by enemies, as the widow was;
   B. There is seeming delay on the part of God.

II. Our Assurance
   A. Persistence wore down a heartless judge;
   B. Our claim on God is great because we are His elect;
   C. We have the promise of the coming of the Son of man.

III. Our Danger
   A. Forgetting our relationship to God;
   B. Loss of faith
      1. Because of the oppression besetting the church;
      2. Because of the delay in the coming of the Son of man.

Conclusion: Marana tha!

THE UNJUST MANAGER
(Luke 16:1-13)

Then for the benefit of His disciples He added: There was a certain man of wealth who had a manager; and this man was accused to him of squandering his property. Then he summoned him and said to him: What is this that I hear about you? Surrender the record of your management; for you can no longer serve as manager. But the manager said within himself: What shall I do, since my master is depriving me of my office and work as steward? I cannot dig; to beg I am ashamed. I know what I will do so that they will take me into their homes when I am removed from office. Then he summoned each one of his master's debtors. He said to the first one, How much do you owe my master? He replied, One hundred measures of olive oil. Then he said to him, Take your bills, sit down and quickly write "fifty." Then he said to the second one: Now, you — how much do you owe? He replied, One hundred measures of wheat. He says to him, Take your papers and write "eighty." And the Lord praised the unjust manager for acting shrewdly; because the children of this world are more shrewd than the sons of light in their dealings each with their own kind. Furthermore, I tell you, make yourselves friends with the mammon of unrighteousness so that, whenever it fails, they may welcome you into the eternal habitations. The man that is faithful in a very small matter is also reliable in an important one; and the man that is unjust in a very small matter is also unrighteous in an important one. Now, if you do not show yourselves to be faithful in the matter of the unrighteous mammon, who will trust you with the true riches? And if you prove yourselves not to be faithful in that which belongs to someone else, who will give you your own? No servant can be a slave of two masters. For either he will hate the one and love the other, or he will cling to the one and despise the other. You cannot serve God and Mammon.

Preliminary Observations:

The parable of the Unjust Manager has often produced nothing short of consternation among Bible readers and interpreters. Julian the Apostate already reproached Christians for the fact that their Lord had chosen the thievish knavery of a cunning rascal as a means of instruction for His disciples (van Koestveld, II, 298). In his commentary on Luke, Klostermann observes that the act of this manager was "a criminal expedient." Creed is of the same opinion in his commentary. Dr. Weinholz, criticizing an article on this parable by Professor Sment in "Evangelisches Gemeindeblatt fuer Rheinland und Westfalen" (1900, No. 37), expressed an opinion which is shared by many: this parable breathes a spirit which "fortunately has not the least resemblance to the spirit of our Lord Jesus, as He speaks to us in the Gospel."

In our *Lectionary* this parable is given as the Gospel for the Ninth Sunday after Trinity. Once a year, therefore, pastor and people hear this story. To many it has been a real *crux interpretum et praedicantium*. Many have been offended by the story. We hardly do justice to such persons by dismissing the whole problem as blithely as Juelicher does (II, 495): "The parable offers no particular difficulty. The grave moral and religious offense . . . exists only for those who are prejudiced." There are chiefly four difficulties in this parable. They are:

1. Where does the parable itself end?

2. Who is the "lord" of 8*a*?
3. Whose is the reason given in 8*b*?
4. Why is conduct which appears to be reprehensible held up as an example for the disciples?

These difficulties, however, are not insuperable, provided we address ourselves to the text for what it says and do so, in the first place, with the understanding of the method and nature of parabolic teaching. "The mere fact that the lesson of prudence is drawn from the life of an unprincipled man is no difficulty to anyone who understands the nature of parabolic teaching" (EGT). Luther remarked (Muehlhaupt, *Luthers Evangelien-Auslegung*, II, 677): "Let us not fall into the error of imagining that everything in the story is significant. If we did, we would be encouraged to go about 'cheating our masters,' as the steward did. No, the point to fasten on is 'the cleverness of the steward who saw his own advantage and so well and wisely achieved it.'"

But that is not saying enough. The really decisive issue in the interpretation of the present parable is the economic practice of that day. Given the background of an understanding of the way in which property was managed in Jesus' day, the prudence of the unjust manager will be found to consist of both forethought and sacrifice. It will become clear that the manager is called "unrighteous" not so much because of the way he manipulated the bills of the tenants but because of the squandering he was accused of at the outset of the story. This whole matter was done very ably and in great detail recently by J. Duncan M. Derrett in "Fresh Light on St. Luke 16," *New Testament Studies* 7:3 (April 1961).

Textual Matters:

V. 1: The δὲ καί is a favorite transitional device of St. Luke. Here the καί goes with ἔλεγεν to show that the parabolic discourse continues from the previous chapter. Actually, as we shall see, this parable is a continuation of the theme started by the Lost Sheep and the Prodigal Son.

Jesus told this particular parable for the benefit of His disciples. This may mean more than the circle of the Twelve. The parables of the previous chapter were apparently told to the scribes and Pharisees. We might note that in v. 14 of the present chapter these same people are depicted as listening in to what Jesus was saying to His disciples.

The Prodigal had squandered his substance. It is perhaps that thought which connects this parable with the previous one. Here is another man who "scattered" goods. In this instance he is a manager of properties. The context, therefore, would suggest that it is squandering that earned this manager the adjective ἄδικος, the word that is picked up in v. 10 for the application.

διεβλήθη is related to the noun from which we have "devil." This is the only time we find the verb used in the N. T. It need not necessarily mean a *false* accusation, although it usually does imply a hostile animus. In this instance the accusation made seems to have been true.

V. 2: τί. This is either an exclamation or an interrogation. It means either, "What! do I hear this of you?" or better, "What is this I hear of you?" In Acts 14:15 is found a similar construction. The verb ἀκούειν can be taken as the passive of λέγειν and mean, "What is this that I am told about you?"

λόγος is the official record or account kept by the manager for his master.

οἰκονομία includes both the activity and the office. It has reference to the distribution (νέμειν) of things. An interesting use of this word is found in Col. 1:25, where Paul applies it to His relationship with God.

V. 3: In Israel death was often thought to be preferable to begging (cf. Ecclus. 40:29-32). Digging ditches was out of the question, probably because the manager was not in a physical condition to join a labor gang.

V. 4: ἔγνων. "I have it; I know now." This is what has been called "the dramatic or tragic aorist." It has much the same sense as the famous εὕρηκα of Archimedes. It describes the result of considerable reflection and concern.

V. 5: ἕνα ἕκαστον. The manager summons each one. Only two instances are given in the subsequent story, enough to show his procedure.

χρεοφειλέτης. Used here and in 7:41. Literally: one who owes a debt.

V. 6: βάτος, not the Greek word as in Luke 6:44, but the Hebrew בַּת (as Ezek. 45:11, where the LXX has χοῖνιξ; 45:14: κοτύλη; Is. 5:10: κεράμιον; 2 Chron. 2:9: μέτρον and κόρος). Like the Hebrew measures, these date from the Babylonian standard of measures. According to Josephus the *batos* was equal to the μετρητής, which is mentioned in John 2:6, in connection with the wedding of Cana. According to present-day measures, one *batos* is equal to 12 gallons. The *koros*, in turn, is equal to 10 *batoi*.

γράψον. This was a matter of writing out a new bill. This bond would be binding on the manager's successor. In this way, too, he used his position to make himself friends for the future.

V. 8: κύριος. There has been an endless amount of discussion as to whether this means our Lord or the master of the parable. Both the KJV and the RSV apply it to the master, presumably to save the reputation of our Lord. Those who take this viewpoint think of the "But I say to you" of the next verse as marking a contrast. But, as Jeremias points out (p. 33), this meaning is nonsensical. How could the master of the parable have praised the manager just after dismissing him? Furthermore, 8b is completely out of place in his mouth. Moreover ὁ κύριος in Luke sometimes refers to God, in other cases (18 times) to Jesus. The analogy of 18:6 suggests that the "lord" is Jesus Himself. Finally, our Lord does (Matt. 10:16) instruct His disciples to be "shrewd," that is, "to grasp the eschatological situation" (Jeremias, p. 34).

V. 9: The καί here reaches back to 8a, in the sense of "also," which gives the καί still greater emphasis. (Cf. Luke 11:9; 20:3; 22:29.)

For δέξωνται cf. 4 Macc. 13:17: "After this fashion, Abraham, Isaac, and Jacob shall receive (ὑποδέξονται) us. . . ." The verb might refer to the friends made with

Mammon. The plural could also be used of the angels, who serve in the presence of God.

For the thought of ἐκλίπῃ cf. Zeph. 1:18: "Neither their silver nor their gold shall be able to deliver them in the day of the Lord's wrath."

"Eternal tents," of course, is a paradox. On the other hand, tents were often considered to be more or less permanent residences, as in the words of the Psalm, "I had rather be a doorkeeper in the house of my Lord than to dwell in the tents of wickedness" (Ps. 84:10). We might also note that dwelling in tents was a feature of the eschatological consummation. (Cf. Acts 15:16 and Mark 9:5.)

μαμονᾶς is a late Hebrew word for money, and probably not connected with any demonology, as was believed in the Middle Ages (Zahn I, p. 295).

V. 13: Very significantly the word οἰκέτης appears here for οἰκονόμος. Of the former there were many in a household; of the latter only one. No doubt that fact accounts for the change to a word with a different meaning but a similar sound and etymological derivation.

Exegetical Items:

This "illustration," as Goodspeed insists on calling the N. T. parables, is not called a parable in the text. But this section is connected with ch. 15; so the word "parable" of 15:3 can carry over.

Nor is it stated in so many words that this parable is intended to present a truth of the kingdom. There can be little doubt, however, of the fact that this is a kingdom parable. The expression "sons of light" (v. 8) would suggest that very strongly.

The thought of squandering, as presented in the Prodigal Son, possibly suggested this parable. Here is a manager who squandered his master's property and so betrayed his trust. For this he is called a "manager of injustice" (v. 8). Note that in v. 10 πιστός and ἄδικος are contrasted directly.

To understand this parable it is imperative to keep in mind that management operated along quite different lines in Jesus' day. A master of that day was normally interested only in getting his fixed portion. Just how this amount was extracted from the tenants was up to the manager.

The manager, in turn, made his living by keeping for himself the difference in the amount that he required from the tenants and that he turned over to the master. In the present instance his arrangement consisted of demanding 100 measures of olive oil from one tenant and keeping 50 for himself. In the second instance he turned over 80 measures.

These sums were fixed by "bonds" (γράμματα). These were written documents to cover the manager's relationship to each tenant. When, therefore, this manager was confronted with the fact that he must relinquish his office, he had various courses of action to follow:
1. He might have handed the bonds over to his master as they were;
2. He could have "squeezed" more out of the tenants

during the last days of his stewardship, to give him something to retire on;

3. He could be generous by sacrificing his own commission and binding the next manager by new bills.

This manager chose the last course of action; and so there is an element of sacrifice in his "prudence." In other words the "manager of unrighteousness" uses the time he still has in office to make himself friends in two ways: by remitting his own commission, and by having more favorable bonds prepared for his tenants. The first man to suggest this explanation was M. Evers in "Das Gleichniss vom ungerechten Haushalter" (1901).

The parable ends at this place; and well it might. For the point has been made that the steward, unjust as he was, used the means at his disposal to make friends who would take him into their homes after his removal from office. His shrewdness was that of a serpent (Matt. 10:16), but in its own sphere it was commendable.

The purpose of the parable is to urge the followers of Christ to similar shrewdness in their dealings with each other. They are to use the means at their disposal toward the purpose of "laying up treasures in heaven."

That is no doubt the emphasis of the parable — not, as Oesterley maintains, consistency in practice. He says, "An important point is the use of parallelisms — both in the parable and in the explanatory comments. These in their *outward form* of ordered consistency illustrate what the parable is intended to teach." (*The Gospel Parables in the Light of their Jewish Background*, p. 195.) He proceeds to explain his point graphically as follows:

These columns must be read downward first:

V. 9: *Making friends of the mammon of unrighteousness* *Being received into everlasting tabernacles*

is being   is the reward of being

V. 10: *Faithful in that which is least;* i. e.,   *Faithful in that which is much;* i. e.,

V. 11: *Being faithful with the unrighteous mammon;*   *Being entrusted with the true riches;*

This from the point of view of the sons of light is   This from the point of view of the sons of light is

V. 12: *That which is another's.*   *That which is your own.*

The principle running through the whole is that of consistency; the conclusion drawn is that no man can serve two masters (v. 13); therefore

YE CANNOT SERVE GOD AND MAMMON

No one will deny that this is an ingenious manner of interpreting the present parable. However, the point that receives most attention, both in the parable and in the Lord's direct statements following the parable proper, is the shrewdness of the steward as such.

The parable was told to the followers of Jesus; and it is clear from vv. 10-12 that Jesus wanted them to know that they, too, were stewards, managers for the great God, their King. The disciples should therefore use the goods entrusted to their stewardship for the purpose of making friends who will receive them into the eternal tabernacles. This certainly means that they are to use God's property to make friends among their own brethren (cf. James 2:15 ff.; 1 John 3:17). They, or God, could be expected to welcome them into the tents of eternity; the sons of this world certainly will not be there to do so, but only the sons of light. The light is an inheritance of the saints (Col. 1:12). The word might also be used of the angels (and of God).

Consequently, when the Lord praises the prudence of the children of the world, he does so not in a general way, but specifically with reference to their relationship to God's gifts entrusted to them. Luther once said that the Christians are "faul, verdrossen, unachtsam, unfleissig in Gottes Sachen." They are too often just that in making use of God's means to make friends for eternity.

The use of the "mammon of unrighteousness" for the benefit of those fellow Christians who are in need will receive its reward in heaven, that is, at the time of death, when mammon will fail (cf. Luke 12:20; 1 Tim. 6:7). For that reason Christian stewards are to plan for that future reception into the tabernacles of eternity and work for that event.

Money is here called the "mammon of unrighteousness," probably because money is really a means invented by men of the world for dealing with each other. It is a means of trafficking used in this world, which is unrighteous in its essence. (Cf. 2 Peter 3:13, where the *new* earth is described as a place where righteousness dwells!) It is used by men of the world for selfish (unrighteous) purposes. Hence the "mammon of unrighteousness" is essentially different from the means which God gives us for daily food and enjoyment (Matt. 5:45; Luke 12: 22-31). Money is the least of all gifts and is given to men for only a short time.

In vv. 10-12 mammon is called "a very small matter," "what belongs to someone else." Opposed to these concepts are the expressions "a large matter," "the true (riches)," "your own."

The latter certainly refer to the knowledge of the way of life, which makes the followers of Christ the children of light. Then the meaning of the last verses would be: "If, therefore, you were not faithful in the use of money, which is really not your own and a very transitory thing, who will trust you with the real thing, the knowledge of life?" Of course the answer is, "No one!" And there is implied the threat uttered at another place (Mark 4:25), "For he that hath, to him shall be given; and he that hath not, from him shall be taken away even that which he hath."

Being unfaithful in the use of mammon makes one a slave of money, and that is not compatible with the position of stewardship in the kingdom of God. Judas was a case in point (John 12:4-6). For that reason Jesus added the last verse, "You cannot serve God and Mammon."

Certainly the parable expresses an important fact of the kingdom rather forcibly; there is no need of resorting to the subtleties of Weiss (in Meyer's commentary), who suggests that there are three distinct appplications in vv. 8-13; one by Jesus (v. 8); one by the compiler of the precanonical Luke (v. 9); and another by Luke himself (vv. 10-13). It is such misguided ingenuity that has distorted this parable and made it seem more difficult than it really is.

This is a favorite pastime of those who look for the "Sitz im Leben" for each parable. They usually concur with the view of Weiss that three applications are made of this parable, not by the Lord but by the church in its later requirements. Much of this approach is very speculative and fails to reckon with the fact that Jesus is, after all, the Lord of the church and could anticipate its problems and its needs. . . .

Says Barnett (*Understanding the Parables of Our Lord*, p. 158): "As a 'son of this age' the manager left no stone unturned to make his future secure. He evaluated the emergency he faced accurately and acted promptly and in terms that under the circumstances were effective to insure a favorable result. The concrete steps he took were unjustifiable by the standards of the Kingdom; and yet his alertness, his immediate and energetic use of opportunity, his aggressive application of the principles in which he believed, his resolution to use the present to determine the future represented a spirit that the 'son of light' might well emulate.

"The point of the parable for Jesus was that the religious man ought to be similarly resourceful in the interest of the values of the Kingdom and in ways that expressed the life of the Kingdom. Zeal, energy, ingeniousness brought to the service of God are at the same premium as when employed for the interest of 'this age.'"

From Derrett's article in *New Testament Studies*, referred to above, we might quote the following five propositions about the steward as being useful for our understanding of the *tertium comparationis:*

1. According to God's law, if the contracts with the debtors had originally been usurious in their nature, he was a sinner in entering into them, and in releasing the debtors from the usurious portion of the debts he was acting righteously and making amends. He was not in fact making restitution, for he had not received this portion as yet; he was doing something better, failing to take the usury to which he was legally entitled.

2. According to God's law, the tainted property did not belong to the master, as he could not authorize the steward to take interest from Jews, and therefore the steward's gain was a personal gain whenever he took usury. Any release of rabbinical usury would, therefore, be a payment out of the steward's own pocket.

3. According to the law of man, however, if the contracts contained rabbinical usury, the steward was perfectly entitled to exact the stipulated amount from the debtors and to sell them and their families into slavery if necessary in order to recover the amount due.

4. According to the law of man the contracts, being legally valid, were entered into on the master's behalf, and in releasing the debts or parts of them to the debtors the steward was depriving the master of something to which he was entitled.

5. According to the law of God as well as the law of man the debtors were entitled to treat the act of the steward in releasing parts of their debts as the act of the master. According to the law of God the steward was doing the righteous thing, and it was presumed that it was his master's wish that he should. According to the law of man it was for the master to prove that he had forbidden the release, or that it was outside the authority of the steward, before the act could be impugned.

Homiletical Suggestions:

Introductory: It is sometimes said that Jesus had nothing to say on how we invest our money. This parable, however, has that as its specific job. It underlines the sobering truth that we are managers for God also in this matter.

INVESTING FOR THE KINGDOM

I. God's Primary Purpose Is to Win People to Serve Him
   1. The church is His activity to gather in His people;
   2. As our King He is also our Master.

II. In This Work We Are His Managers
   1. Our parable describes this relationship;
   2. God is the giver of all good things;
   3. There is therefore an account with Him.

www.ingramcontent.com/pod-product-compliance
Lightning Source LLC
Chambersburg PA
CBHW032132090426
42743CB00007B/570